CONTENTS

INIQUITY

HOW COURT SYSTEMS, ATTORNEYS, AND LEGAL AID ORGANIZATIONS CHEATED HOMEOWNERS IN FORECLOSURE

Kelli Dudley

Contact for reprints and permissions:
attorneykelli@sbcglobalnet

Updates and corrections available: www.kellidudley.com

Many thanks to volunteer editors, including my mother. The remaining errors are mine. Please check for updates and corrections: www.kellidudley.com A mailing list is available.

There are not words for the sacrifices my family has made. Oftentimes, my desire to help those most in need has resulted in no income and a slew of expenses. My longsuffering benefactor, David, has made my continued existence possible, has urged me to continue to choose worthy endeavors, and has sacrificed time and money. Without him, I would choose a more financially profitable path. Without him, I would have no humanity. He has provided me the luxury of depositing all my decency and goodness in one place, echoing it back to me when needed. His own talents have gone unrecognized in service to what, I hope, has been a great undertaking that will, someday, yield a just result.

My grandfather lives in everything I do. I am a pale reflection of his love for people, animals, and justice.

I cannot see a footnote or citations without thinking of the meticulous work of my anthropology mentor, Hilda Pang. For my nearly lifelong friend and mentor Ruth Brookshire, I can only say I truly regret that she is not here. My living friends and mentors know who they are and will recognize themselves whether explicitly mentioned or not. Many living mentors and friends have been passed over in an effort to avoid incurring, for them, the vitriol of petty tyrants. There will be reprisals for this book, and I hope to limit the number of concrete shoes to the pair reserved for me.

Often bearing the brunt of my schedule and work have been my many furry companions. They have comforted me as I mourned brutality they could not comprehend and of the type the non-human animal world cannot muster.

This is published on my 29th anniversary with David and the fourth anniversary of the day my beloved dog slipped peacefully out of this world. The comfort one oddly-shaped, yet remarkably dapper, dog brought directly to crying clients lives on, as does his relentless support of me as I fought evil beyond his comprehension.

OPENING ARGUMENT

"Could I write all, the world would turn to stone."*Caterina Sforza*

It was hard to step away from fighting genocide (taking someone's home away and isolating them in a racially-homogenous neighborhood being a brilliant way to kill a targeted population, such as poor people or black people, over time) to write this book, but it called out to be written. In over fifteen years of substantively defending foreclosures, fighting fraud, and representing poor people and others relegated to the sidelines, I have made a lot of enemies. The system has become so unable (or unwilling) to help that arguments in court often become counterproductive--resulting in unwarranted threats of sanctions or even screaming fits unrelated to the merits of the case. Court proceedings in Cook County are not presently recorded (by transcription or by audio recording--although recordings have been promised to resume in some divisions in 2019), so the public has little access to some of the fantastical goings-on. This book modestly offers to crack the courthouse doors just a little on some of the most upsetting deprivations of homeowners' rights in foreclosure. For every frustration expressed in this book, there are a hundred related to other areas of law. Tenants are unfairly kicked out of their homes, alleged debtors are treated as organ-grinding monkeys, and those accused of crimes are too often tortured, humiliated, and murdered. This is without mentioning immigration, which stands alone--an exemplar of the justice system's increasing lack of humanity.

The past few years have taught me how far people will go to pre-serve the *status quo* even when it does not seem to benefit them. Working people a paycheck away from foreclosure will fight to defend the "right" of lenders to carelessly foreclose. Plaintiff's foreclosure attorneys often make less money, at least during their first few years of practice, than many working people. They are often less financially secure than those whose homes they seek to take. The same is true for many process servers, Sheriff's officers, court clerks, notaries, and board-up workers. Nonetheless, they often cut corners and curtail homeowners' rights without apol-ogy. Foreclosure complaints are so badly written, in many cases at some firms, that only entry-level lawyers will risk their law licenses by affixing their professional signature to a packet of im-aginative, if not delusional, text.

Other attorneys argue they "need the money" as an excuse for atrocious behavior. Curiously, those who make it to the upper echelons and gloat about their income, savings, and lifestyle are as protective of their jobs at large foreclosure firms (referred to in the pejorative as "mills" by some foreclosure "defense" lawyers--many of whom who would do well to take greater care with their own clients). Even having the greatest first-hand knowledge of the fraud perpetrated by the rescue scammers who prey on those in foreclosure, they largely refuse to testify when a homeowner has the courage (and a willing lawyer) to ask the courts for redress for the harm caused by rescue fraud. The firms, in some cases, re-strict their employees' ability to testify to bare facts they have seen. It is hard to understand why anyone, much less a highly-qualified attorney, would willingly be disenfranchised for a pay-check.

Of course, plaintiffs' attorneys have limited culpability. After all, they are the wolves at the door, and they largely present themselves as wolves. One facing foreclosure is usually aware the bank's lawyer is not the homeowners' lawyer and can make decisions accordingly.

In contrast, there are many wolves in sheep's clothing, parading under the "save your home" banner. For example, some nonprofit organizations are interested primarily in money and do anything to protect their turf. It bears remembering that the non-profit status prevents an organization from accruing profit to be paid out to shareholders in the way a corporation does. Non-profit status is not an indicia of honesty, integrity, competence, or goodness. Non-profit organizations can pay inflated salaries and do little to benefit the community, just as corporations can, conversely, choose to operate more compassionately. Many use "non profit" as a shibboleth, and this is completely unwarranted and counterproductive. This book discusses efforts to undermine zealous advocates and avoid raising the standard of foreclosure defense law to one of requiring a zealous legal defense. However, nonprofits sometimes behave in simply silly ways even outside of the foreclosure context, as in the case of a large, well-funded fair housing center that promised to support me in a significant *pro bono* fair housing case. The staff absconded with all my clients' paperwork, multiplying my work, and sent their lawyer to (albeit laughably) attempt to intimidate me when I issued a subpoena for my clients' own paperwork.

Perhaps most illustrative of the off-course turn nonprofit advocacy has taken is a relatively minor incident from the case above. My clients faced eviction from their homes for allegedly violating municipal ordinances, a matter decided in an administrative hearing presided over by a judge (hearing officer) contracted by the municipality. Another enormously funded non-profit legal aid organization abruptly quit representing the homeowners with no notice whatsoever, leaving several to be evicted without even an attempt at a defense. The organization filed no motion to withdraw, wrote no letter to any client, and made no contact with opposing counsel; the lawyer who abandoned the clients later told me, "There's nothing you can do at an administrative hearing anyway." Despite this warning, I stepped into the case and prepared defenses, bracing to file appeals if needed. At that point, another lawyer (this one working for the well-funded fair housing center mentioned above) called me to chastise me for asking for a ride for a witness. The organization had volunteered help with logistics, but, according to this highly-paid lawyer, "You don't need a witness at an administrative hearing because you can't do anything." In fact, I accomplished a lot for the group of clients in question (and used at least two non-party witnesses-- transporting them myself--in the process), but these clients were not in foreclosure and their success story is not part of this book. These examples illustrate the very, very little that those who earn steady salaries to help those in need are willing to do in many cases and how bizarrely compelled they seem to be to interfere with those who do work hard for their clients. It seems that collecting a paycheck for no or little work would be enough. On the day I die, I will remain baffled by those who are well paid to fight for housing and yet turn away from the opportunity to help those most in need, even interfering with those fighting this uphill battle.

Some of my questions about motivations were answered when the non-profit organization mentioned above offered two people board memberships in exchange for not consorting with me. One dropped a volunteer case in which he represented people who were evicted at gunpoint rather than using the legal process to cash in on this seemingly meagre lucre. Another degraded her law license by serving on the board and then having herself hired (a blatant conflict of interest that should cost the organization its "non-profit" status--but won't).

Of course, writing this book is, in part, a telling of my personal story. This would probably have been lost--and maybe not a great loss--but for one incident. A public diatribe against me by a former judge made it necessary to me to correct the record.

While I have never been a perfect lawyer, I have tried to be a good one, consistently taking on cases that were considered difficult. I never wanted to work in an area of law where I would fill out forms or print out complaints with the same four or five factual recitations every day. I sought to help those who were turned away because of the combination of poverty and complexity.

One area of law I developed was a theory that people who were scammed by "save your home" lawyers could sue under the Fair Housing Act if they were targeted based on a protected status like race. I was not entirely alone in this belief. A few fair housing organizations across the country teamed up with large law firms to sue foreclosure rescue firms. The Illinois Attorney General brought a case using a format very similar to mine.

I met a couple scammed because they were immigrants. The scam violated the FHA's prohibition on discrimination based on national origin. The scammer spoke their language to earn trust. The scam was so vile that it involved stealing the deed to the home and taking monthly fees and attorney fees for the privilege of having the home stolen. However, the court was skeptical that this "targeting" (providing a toxic service to the ethnic group rather than denying them a service) violated the FHA. The district court judge wrote a reasonable opinion. Even though I believed it was incorrect, I did not find it or the judge insulting or demeaning to me or my clients. Disagreement is something lawyers and judges do. In this case, my clients and I had been subject to demeaning language, but certainly not from the judge. Initially, most of the demeaning language came from the opposing counsel, a petty little man who slimed through the court system to, seemingly, illustrate the legal profession's neglect of its duty to regulate itself. His missives to me included asking why "in your [my] crazy mind" certain legal language was included in my pleadings. He died a sad and broken man, leaving behind tacky condominiums in a fancy zip codes as well as a pending petition for bankruptcy protection. Though the lawyer claimed to defend foreclosures, the banks' efforts to lift the bankruptcy stay with respect to his bankruptcy petition reflect a legacy almost as sad and broken as his life.

When I appealed the case, it should have been overturned. Alternatively, the court could have simply affirmed it, using recognized legal language.

Oral argument was heard on the case. I argued and made substantive legal points relating to the case. The opposing counsel sent a young lawyer who virtually screamed loud, declarative sentences devoid of any legal substance or grammatical structure. The lawyer was supported by a bevy of young fraternity cohorts who giggled throughout my argument and left the courtroom screaming "liar" so loud it echoed through downtown Chicago (and made loud declarations of the same when it was my turn to address the court). This behavior was a radical departure from the court's normal decorum, but was never addressed.

It was unlikely I would be the bad actor in a case where my opposing counsel screamed "Liar!" and seemed to think volume mattered over substance in court. However, a former judge penned an opinion saying I lied. My lie went to a question as to whether a pleading had been amended. At oral argument, I thought the judge asked if I had amended the foreclosure answer in the state court-- a step I often struggled to be able to take effectively for my clients in spite of significant legal barriers to doing so. I answered "no." In the opinion, the judge said the question was whether my Federal complaint had been amended. While it technically had, if that was the question, I had made no substantive amendment, only adding an exhibit to appease an opposing counsel who was too lazy to read Federal Rule of Civil Procedure 10. The most correct answer would also have been "No, not substantively." "No" was not a lie in either case.

After this vitriol, penned by a former judge who proclaims himself the leading public intellectual in the United States, I knew my side of the story--and my clients' stories--had to come out.

I had a volunteer editor for this book, and my mother edited it. One facet of the Chicago legal community that comes out in the book is the parochial level of thinking. Most of Chicago lawyers seem to absorb only a technical education about law. Many are loathe to sustain a conversation, having no grasp of literature, culture, the arts, or cuisine lacking mustard and a bun.

Should any of those lawyers decide to attempt to humiliate me, as did the dead excuse for a lawyer mentioned above when he cited, in a legal brief, my telling of an anecdote about Caterina Sforza as evidence of . . . my poor morals? my promiscuity? One cannot even imagine what was in his sad little mind . . . . Anyway, even my mother already knows. She has known me for fifty years. She edited the book.

My work is made possible by a benefactor who lets me live with him and keeps me in vegan ice cream. He doesn't look the part and is best described as "not a man, but a mystery." Attempts to come between us are not likely to succeed. He likes the Sforza anecdote.

I suggest any detractors eat their hot dogs and try to make their own mortgage payments on time. Names and facts are changed, condensed, fictionalized, and shuffled. The same fact pattern occurs so often in my office, the banks and scammers not being too awfully creative, that fact patterns come in, at least, pairs. They are beyond recognizability compared to real cases, even to me, as written here.

In short, take this book with a grain of salt, as fiction. Maybe everything is fine. Maybe our city blocks are not full of boarded up, vacant homes.

INTRODUCTION

Why I Did It

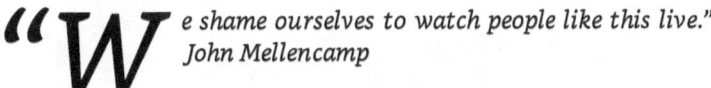

"**W**e shame ourselves to watch people like this live."
John Mellencamp

Not too many people ask me why I did what I did. People in Chicago care a great deal about your ethnicity and race, and I get lots of questions about my accent and appearance. It all fits into the subtle calculus of whether your presence indicates a "changing" neighborhood and the attendant need to move to a new sprawling, poorly-constructed subdivision of future foreclosures. But they do not ask about my motivation. I guess they assume I defended people who were losing their homes for money—a losing proposition, and, now that I think about, possibly why so many of them thought I was stupid. People in Chicago are motivated by gluttony and racism (not necessarily in that order), and, by those standards, I failed.

So I'll tell you: I never tried to be anything other than the attorney my grandparents and great-grandparents should have had. Our family lost two homes between 1911 and 1945 or so. I know the dates because the homes were lost after my grandfather was born and before he showed up in Indiana and built a home still owned by our family today. The first loss was probably a taking for the purpose of getting coal from under the family farm in Ona, Cabell County, West Virginia, and the second loss was likely due to eminent domain; our populated place (not a village or town), Waltz, Rowan County, Kentucky, is right in the middle of the Daniel Boone National Forest. Kentucky took farms for the park; those who fought largely lost cases like *Kentucky Nat. Park Commission ex rel. Commonwealth v. Russell*, 301 Ky. 187 (Ky. Ct. App. 1945). The area where my family lived and farmed is divided by park land and roads, but was once laced with gravel roads and paths leading from one home to another. Two were owned by my grandfather and his parents. Exhibit A shows the little church, Old Sardis Church, where our family is buried.

Exhibit A, Old Sardis Church, Cranston, Rowan County, Kentucky (burned 2016 and since rebuilt)

I don't know all the details of how my Grandpa's homes were taken. He was born in an area so remote that it was several years before his birth certificate was registered. Records are not always easily accessible. And the records for his second home are in Rowan County, Kentucky, home to a vile clerk recently unseated after gaining notoriety for refusing to issue marriage licenses to gay couples. I am good at looking the devil in the eye and asking for what I need, but I have limits.

Since the writing of this book, the clerk mentioned above has been defeated and I have undertaken a trip home to decorate graves and will soon return for the arduous task of finding out what really happened to our land. However, the location of our area--right in the middle of national park--makes it likely it was an eminent domain case.

It may be 100 years too late to save family homes lost states away, but the pain still lingers. One of my favorite pictures shows my Grandpa, Grandma, and Aunt Beulah in front of a rotted-out structure—the old home place. They face the camera, turning away from their former home in Kentucky, bewildered at the destruction and heartbroken, heading toward their car after a detour on a visit to the cemetery. My Grandma often said her only regret was not being able to fit her Victrola in the car for the move north; I suspect she regretted much more. Another family picture shows my grandparents and their children with a truck several years after their move north. I know my Grandpa mourned the loss of his homes and developed a mistrust of banks that caused him to build a spot to hide money in the wall of his Indiana home. He once bought something in cash, just to have the banker counting it comment on how truly cold his cold, hard cash was. It was cold, having been hidden away for years in the walls, nestled into the foundation of the house he built and owned.

The mistrust of banks followed Grandpa to his grave. He lived in the Indiana home he built until he died, and the home is still in our family. By the time I came along, Grandpa was nearing retirement. We often passed our days fishing—he fished, I brought along books and read. Some of our greatest times together were trips back to Kentucky for Decoration (Memorial) Day. Somewhere between old home places and rescuing animals we found together, Grandpa imparted the message that everyone deserved a home— but one could not rely on bankers to make that happen.

The destruction and heartbreak of those who have lost their homes are familiar to me as an adult. I have seen them in the neighborhoods of Chicago and in the eyes of my clients. I fought to be the lawyer my grandparents should have had, and, some of the time, I succeeded. Some lawyers spend time in books and reading about the Constitution, developing subtle arguments that earn praise and advance big-picture causes. Well-funded legal clinics that claim to operate on a non-profit basis crow about their "impact cases," as if every case does not have an impact in someone's life.

In contrast, I got to know the contours of poverty and desperation—presenting arguments that were more pleas for mercy than novel legal arguments. Most of the time, my opponent was a system that devalued hearth and home. Often, my opposing counsel were sympathetic people one paycheck away from foreclosure themselves (and several became clients or referred their family members to me over the years). The system refused to recognize defenses to foreclosure, even when I was right—and even after my arguments won. In fact, winning arguments were often met with legislative changes—elected representatives eagerly bowing to the monied interests who instigated financial crises rather than allowing laws to be enforced to the benefit of homeowners. One of the best examples was the legislative response to motions to quash. Homeowners are often not properly served with process (a copy of the summons and complaint informing them of the foreclosure lawsuit against them). Process servers regularly leave the paperwork under doormats or stuck in door jambs despite legal requirements it be given to the defendant or a member of their household directly. Bringing this problem to judges was so often successful that the legislature adopted a special law [735 ILCS 5/1505.6(a)] stripping people in foreclosure of due process rights. Even if a homeowner is not served with the paperwork, this fact cannot be asserted in court after sixty days from when the homeowner "participates" in the case. *Wells Fargo Bank v. Roundtree*, 2018 IL App (1st) 172912 (Nov. 7, 2018). Essentially, the courts, using this law, exercise jurisdiction over those who have not been served under the law, taking away their homes without due process. This law provides for one narrow group—people accused of breaching their mortgage agreement—to be deprived of a cornerstone of the Constitution, due process. Due process, understood as providing a defendant with a copy of a summons and complaint in a way set forth by law, is an old concept and enforced in every other kind of case. In other words, in the United States, outside of foreclosure cases in Illinois for the past few years, it is unconstitutional to take away someone's rights, including property rights, if they are known (as homeowners always are, since, as mortgage companies love to point out, they signed the mortgage) without properly notifying them of the action against them and allowing a meaningful opportunity to respond. One such old case decided by the U.S. Supreme Court is *Mullane v. Central Hanover Bank & Trust Co.*, 339 U.S. 306 (1950).

Advice Desk

I stumbled into defending foreclosures. My original plan was to set up a solo practice suing insurance companies that wrongfully refuse to investigate or pay the claims of their insured. During law school, I began working for the South Chicago Legal Clinic, a clinic begun to serve those affected by the rising poverty and unemployment resulting from steel mill closures on the south side of Chicago. The Clinic's main office was in South Chicago, an urban neighborhood comprised of black and Latinx residents who still view each other with enough suspicion to be *bona fide* Chicagoans. Through 2017, it was ably run by one of its founders, Edward ("Ed") Grossman. Ed and co-founder, Bishop Thomas Paprocki, will always be the founders of the Clinic and the motivators of all the good it has done. They intentionally located the Clinic in an economically hard-hit neighborhood to increase the comfort level of clients rather than bowing to the prejudices of some staff or catering to the misperceptions of the powers that be with a downtown address. The South Chicago address remained the headquarters throughout the organization's existence.

I met Ed on September 11, 2001. Mine was the only car headed into the city as even the lackadaisical public transit to Indiana ran extra train cars to evacuate downtown Chicago. Phone lines were down, so I was unable to confirm the seeming likelihood that my job interview was canceled. I arrived amazed to find Ed, and most of the staff, hard at work. Ed sat at a reception desk greeting visitors, leading me to initially believe he was the receptionist. After my interview, Ed handed me a pile of folders and asked if I could start that day. Because I was unsure where my husband was—and this was before everyone had a cell phone—I begged off and began three days later.

Part of my work at the Clinic involved helping those who did not fit neatly into the Clinic's established programs. Ed was the Executive Director (not the receptionist), and I worked for him, so I got the cases that landed on his desk. Many of these were foreclosures. The default position among the bar was that those facing foreclosure could sell or refinance their homes. Little work was done, at that time, defending the homes. However, foreclosures were increasing. It became clear that new approaches were needed.

In response to this need, Ed began working with the then-Presiding Judge of the Chancery Division of the Circuit Court of Cook County, Lester Foreman, and a private lawyer, Harold Levine, to plan a Chancery Advice Desk. Unfortunately, both Judge Foreman and Mr. Levine died before I could meet them.

After law school graduation, I was prepared to leave the Clinic. My plan to set up a small firm to help those whose insurance claims were neglected was moving ahead, fueled by my own run-ins with insurance companies over the years. However, as I packed my box to go to the closet I planned to rent for office space, I got a call from Ed. He wanted me to stick around to start the Chancery Advice Desk, giving brief advice to people in foreclosure. I agreed. However, given my history (I had never had a "job" I liked.), I extracted an agreement that I could leave with no hard feelings after two years (and left after a small, friendly battle after three).

When we started the Chancery Advice Desk in 2004, we thought we were in a crisis. We served about 1,300 people that first year

—and thought that was phenomenal. We were still a couple of years away from the crash, when foreclosure would climb closer and closer to 81,000 cases pending in the Circuit Court of Cook County each year.

The desk was a collaboration between the private lawyers, bar associations, the Court, and legal service organizations such as the Clinic. I worked for the Clinic, but the Presiding Judge of the Chancery Division of the Court, Dorothy Kinnaird, fought tirelessly for improvements and was a benevolent and fair advocate for meaningful access to the court system. Judge Kinnaird was a devoted presence. She set firm timelines for designing the layout of the desk area, procured space in the courthouse, and—once the desk opened—would summon me to a courtroom to help a confused litigant on the spot.

The desk opened on Valentine's Day, 2004. I had requested the Cook County procurement officer who helped us furnish the desk to deliver the key on a heart key ring—and he did! At times, clients would trickle in. At other times, there would be a deluge, making it difficult for me to attend court dates or keep commitments to other clients. The main source of referrals was judges, desperate for something to say to the fearful and, often, angry litigants who came before them.

The Desk initially had three volunteers. Two were young women from out-of-state law schools who, lacking the connections that sometimes accompany graduation from a local school, wanted to enhance their resumes. In Chicago, they still don't want nobody nobody sent (to paraphrase the words uttered to storied Judge Abner Mikva when, as a young man, he tried to volunteer for a political campaign and was turned away when he said "nobody" sent him). Reluctance to hire based on qualifications persists even though patronage and nepotism are shown over and again to fail, sometimes resulting in prison sentences. Large firms and well-heeled non profits often will not grant interviews to the most talented young lawyers. Getting a reference from someone like Ed was invaluable for volunteers as they sought jobs. The third was a cheerful young man who made the mistake of stopping into the Clinic office while I was there alone during a lunch hour. He was dropping off a package for my boss, to whom he referred as Eddie. I only knew one group of people who called Ed "Eddie": his family. I asked which cousin he was, and he described a long-standing friendship. After watching me dribble Thai food down my blouse, he remained a good friend. He was a right-hand of sorts on the desk, trustworthy, and remains a treasured colleague today. I won't let anyone consider a bankruptcy without first consulting Butch.

Although I understood the Desk was somewhat controversial (after all, the banks benefitted from having homeowners confused and without help), I was not prepared for what we encountered. Even before the Desk opened, a public service lawyer said I lacked the experience to make the desk a success. He commented upon my qualifications, yet he did not want the job himself. Nor did he offer the Desk any assistance. Then, a foreclosure firm sent in a "spy" during our first week. The young attorney posed as someone needing help in a laughable endeavor to steal our nonexistent playbook. When I later recognized her, she tried to become "muscle" in a laughable attempt to intimidate me.

As the Desk saw its first patrons,[1] it began identifying patterns of procedural inadequacy, which formed the basis for several groundbreaking documents that could then be tailored to each client and their unique situation and enabled attorneys to provide meaningful assistance to people facing foreclosure. First, attorneys for the banks routinely failed to attach the mortgage and note being foreclosed upon to the foreclosure complaint, despite Paragraph 1 of the standard Illinois foreclosure complaint stating that the mortgage is attached to the complaint as Exhibit A and the note as Exhibit B. We began doing motions to dismiss for failure to attach the documents. The motion was not just technical—we had trouble analyzing the complaints and determining if the amounts asserted owed by the homeowners were correct without the underlying documents. When I pointed out this rather dull procedural error, plaintiffs' attorneys became rattled. After about six months, one tried to reach a blanket agreement with me that I would stop objecting on this basis. I suggested I would stop objecting if the plaintiffs simply followed the rules and attached the required paperwork. The Illinois Mortgage Foreclosure Law (IMFL) has a sample complaint written by the legislature as part of the statute. It was reasonable to ask plaintiff's bar to comply with the very minimal legal requirements that must be met before taking someone's home in Illinois.

The standard IMFL complaint is simple and provides a form for foreclosing plaintiffs to complete. The various line items even include instructions advising lawyers what information they should insert. The sample and instructions are set forth at 735 ILCS 5/15-1504, but I am including it here to illustrate how far the Illinois legislature went in doing the work of foreclosure plaintiffs for them. Areas plaintiffs commonly disregard or fill with fantastical allegations are in bold print.

Sec. 15-1504. Pleadings and service.

(a) Form of Complaint. A foreclosure complaint may be in substantially the following form:

(1) Plaintiff files this complaint to foreclose the mortgage (or other conveyance in the nature of a mortgage) (hereinafter called "mortgage") hereinafter described and joins the following person as defendants: (here insert names of all defendants).

(2) Attached as Exhibit "A" is a copy of the mortgage and as Exhibit "B" is a copy of the note secured thereby.

(3) Information concerning mortgage:

(A) Nature of instrument: (here insert whether a
mortgage, trust deed or other instrument in the nature of a mortgage,
etc.)
(B) Date of mortgage:
(C) Name of mortgagor:
(D) Name of mortgagee:
(E) Date and place of recording:
(F) Identification of recording: (here insert
book and page number or document number)
(G) Interest subject to the mortgage: (here insert whether fee simple,
estate for years, undivided interest, etc.)
(H) Amount of original indebtedness, including
subsequent advances made under the mortgage:
(I) Both the legal description of the mortgaged
real estate and the common address or other information sufficient
to identify it with reasonable certainty:
(J) Statement as to defaults, including, but not
necessarily limited to, date of default, current unpaid principal
balance, per diem interest accruing, and any further information
concerning the default:
(K) Name of present owner of the real estate:
(L) Names of other persons who are joined as
defendants and whose interest in or lien on the mortgaged real estate is
sought to be terminated:
(M) Names of defendants claimed to be personally
liable for deficiency, if any:
(N) Capacity in which plaintiff brings this
foreclosure (here indicate whether plaintiff is the legal holder of the
indebtedness, a pledgee, an agent, the trustee under a trust deed or
otherwise, as appropriate):
(O) Facts in support of redemption period shorter
than the longer of (i) 7 months from the date the mortgagor or, if more
than one, all the mortgagors (I) have been served with summons or by
publication or (II) have otherwise submitted to the jurisdiction of the

court, or (ii) 3 months from the entry of the judgment of foreclosure, if sought (here indicate whether based upon the real estate not being residential or real estate value less than 90% of amount owed, etc.):

(P) Statement that the right of redemption has been waived by all owners of redemption, if applicable:

(Q) Facts in support of request for attorneys' fees and of costs and expenses, if applicable:

(R) Facts in support of a request for appointment of mortgagee in possession or for appointment of receiver, and identity of such receiver, if sought:

(S) Offer to mortgagor in accordance with Section 15-1402 to accept title to the real estate in satisfaction of all indebtedness and obligations secured by the mortgage without judicial sale, if sought:

(T) Name or names of defendants whose right to possess the mortgaged real estate, after the confirmation of a foreclosure sale, is sought to be terminated and, if not elsewhere stated, the facts in support thereof:

REQUEST FOR RELIEF

Plaintiff requests:

(i) A judgment of foreclosure and sale.

(ii) An order granting a shortened redemption period, if sought.

(iii) A personal judgment for a deficiency, if sought.

(iv) An order granting possession, if sought.

(v) An order placing the mortgagee in possession or appointing a receiver, if sought.

(vi) A judgment for attorneys' fees, costs and expenses, if sought.

❖ ❖ ❖

Because the legislature provides a pre-written form, plaintiffs in foreclosure are relieved of almost all legal work associated with any case. However, compounding difficulties for homeowners and further facilitating easy taking of homes, the Illinois legislature has included a caveat that, once the above form complaint is filed, other information, not set forth in writing in any place to inform the homeowner it is included, is "deemed" part of the complaint. If the homeowner fails to answer these "deemed" allegations despite their invisibility, the allegations are "deemed" admitted by the homeowner and can support entry of judgment in favor of the bank. The deemed (secret) allegations are set forth below, part of 735 ILCS 5/2-1504:

(c) Allegations. The statements contained in a complaint in the form set forth in subsection (a) of Section 15-1504 are deemed and construed to include allegations as follows:

(1) that, on the date indicated, the obligor of the indebtedness or other obligations secured by the mortgage was justly indebted in the amount of the indicated original indebtedness to the original mortgagee or payee of the mortgage note;
(2) that the exhibits attached are true and correct copies of the mortgage and note and are incorporated and made a part of the complaint by express reference;
(3) that the mortgagor was at the date indicated an owner of the interest in the real estate described in the complaint and that as of that date made, executed and delivered the mortgage as security for the note or other obligations;
(4) that the mortgage was recorded in the county in which the mortgaged real estate is located, on the date indicated, in the book and page or as the document number indicated;
(5) that defaults occurred as indicated;
(6) that at the time of the filing of the complaint

the persons named as present owners are the owners of the indicated interests in and to the real estate described;

(7) that the mortgage constitutes a valid, prior and paramount lien upon the indicated interest in the mortgaged real estate, which lien is prior and superior to the right, title, interest, claim or lien of all parties and nonrecord claimants whose interests in the mortgaged real estate are sought to be terminated;

(8) that by reason of the defaults alleged, if the indebtedness has not matured by its terms, the same has become due by the exercise, by the plaintiff or other persons having such power, of a right or power to declare immediately due and payable the whole of all indebtedness secured by the mortgage;

(9) that any and all notices of default or election to declare the indebtedness due and payable or other notices required to be given have been duly and properly given;

(10) that any and all periods of grace or other period of time allowed for the performance of the covenants or conditions claimed to be breached or for the curing of any breaches have expired;

(11) that the amounts indicated in the statement in the complaint are correctly stated and if such statement indicates any advances made or to be made by the plaintiff or owner of the mortgage indebtedness, that such advances were, in fact, made or will be required to be made, and under and by virtue of the mortgage the same constitute additional indebtedness secured by the mortgage; and

(12) that, upon confirmation of the sale, the holder of the certificate of sale or deed issued pursuant to that certificate or, if no certificate or deed was issued, the purchaser at the sale will be entitled to full possession of the mortgaged real estate against the parties named in clause (T) of paragraph (3) of subsection (a) of Section 15-1504 or elsewhere to the same effect; the omission of any party indicates that plaintiff will not seek a possessory order in the order confirming sale unless the request is subsequently made under subsection (h) of Section 15-1701 or by separate action under Article 9 of this Code.

(d) Request for Fees and Costs. A statement in the complaint that plaintiff seeks the inclusion of attorneys' fees and of costs and expenses shall be deemed and construed to include allegations that:

(1) plaintiff has been compelled to employ and retain attorneys to prepare and file the complaint and to represent and advise the plaintiff in the foreclosure of the mortgage and the plaintiff will thereby become liable for the usual, reasonable and customary fees of the attorneys in that behalf;

(2) the plaintiff has been compelled to advance or will be compelled to advance, various sums of money in payment of costs, fees, expenses and disbursements incurred in connection with the foreclosure, including, without limiting the generality of the foregoing, filing fees, stenographer's fees, witness fees, costs of publication, costs of procuring and preparing documentary evidence and costs of procuring abstracts of title, Torrens certificates, foreclosure minutes and a title insurance policy;

(3) under the terms of the mortgage, all such advances, costs, attorneys' fees and other fees, expenses and disbursements are made a lien upon the mortgaged real estate and the plaintiff is entitled to recover all such advances, costs, attorneys' fees, expenses and disbursements, together with interest on all advances at the rate provided in the mortgage, or, if no rate is provided therein, at the statutory judgment rate, from the date on which such advances are made;

(4) in order to protect the lien of the mortgage, it may become necessary for plaintiff to pay taxes and assessments which have been or may be levied upon the mortgaged real estate;

(5) in order to protect and preserve the mortgaged real estate, it may also become necessary for the plaintiff to pay liability (protecting mortgagor and mortgagee), fire and other hazard insurance premiums on the mortgaged real estate, make such repairs to the mortgaged real estate as may reasonably be deemed necessary for the proper preservation thereof, advance for costs to inspect the mortgaged real estate or to appraise it, or both, and advance for premiums for pre-existing private or governmental mortgage insurance to the extent required after a foreclosure is commenced in order to keep such insur-

ance in force; and

(6) under the terms of the mortgage, any money so paid or expended will become an additional indebtedness secured by the mortgage and will bear interest from the date such monies are advanced at the rate provided in the mortgage, or, if no rate is provided, at the statutory judgment rate.

(e) Request for Foreclosure. The request for foreclosure is deemed and construed to mean that the plaintiff requests that:

(1) an accounting may be taken under the direction of the court of the amounts due and owing to the plaintiff;

(2) the defendants be ordered to pay to the plaintiff before expiration of any redemption period (or, if no redemption period, before a short date fixed by the court) whatever sums may appear to be due upon the taking of such account, together with attorneys' fees and costs of the proceedings (to the extent provided in the mortgage or by law);

(3) in default of such payment in accordance with the judgment, the mortgaged real estate be sold as directed by the court, to satisfy the amount due to the plaintiff as set forth in the judgment, together with the interest thereon at the statutory judgment rate from the date of the judgment;

(4) in the event the plaintiff is a purchaser of the mortgaged real estate at such sale, the plaintiff may offset against the purchase price of such real estate the amounts due under the judgment of foreclosure and order confirming the sale;

(5) in the event of such sale and the failure of any person entitled thereto to redeem prior to such sale pursuant to this Article, the defendants made parties to the foreclosure in accordance with this Article, and all nonrecord claimants given notice of the foreclosure in accordance with this Article, and all persons claiming by, through or under them, and each and any and all of them, may be forever barred and foreclosed of any right, title, interest, claim, lien, or right to redeem in and to the mortgaged real estate; and

(6) if no redemption is made prior to such sale, a

deed may be issued to the purchaser thereat according to law and such purchaser be let into possession of the mortgaged real estate in accordance with Part 17 of this Article.

(f) Request for Deficiency Judgment. A request for a personal judgment for a deficiency in a foreclosure complaint if the sale of the mortgaged real estate fails to produce a sufficient amount to pay the amount found due, the plaintiff may have a personal judgment against any party in the foreclosure indicated as being personally liable therefor and the enforcement thereof be had as provided by law.

(g) Request for Possession or Receiver. A request for possession or appointment of a receiver has the meaning as stated in subsection (b) of Section 15-1706.

(h) Answers by Parties. Any party may assert its interest by counterclaim and such counterclaim may at the option of that party stand in lieu of answer to the complaint for foreclosure and all counter complaints previously or thereafter filed in the foreclosure. Any such counterclaim shall be deemed to constitute a statement that the counter claimant does not have sufficient knowledge to form a belief as to the truth or falsity of the allegations of the complaint and all other counterclaims, except to the extent that the counterclaim admits or specifically denies such allegations.

It is hard to imagine any other area of law where the legislature would do the work of writing a complaint, in advance, for highly-paid attorneys representing moneyed interests. They certainly do not subsidize the fraud and consumer litigation needed by consumers in this way. However, even with this boost from the legislature, foreclosure attorneys often refused to comply with simple requirements.

Consistent with the above, homeowners can be "deemed" to have admitted that correct copies of their mortgage and note were attached to the complaint, even where nothing was attached. Likewise, people not named in the complaint ("'non-record" parties) can be deprived of all due process.

At the Advice Desk, we began writing thorough answers and objecting when plaintiffs seeking to take homes did not comply with the minimal procedural requirements applicable to foreclosure cases.

Next, we began objecting when homeowners were not served. Service of process was (and, despite efforts of the courts to accommodate the foreclosure plaintiffs' laziness, still is) often "sewer service." Documents were often not served in-hand as required by law, but a copy of the complaint was simply sent via mail, left under a door mat, or stuck in the door. Naturally, the frightened homeowners would run into court without a lawyer and inadvertently submit to the court's jurisdiction without being afforded the minimum due process demanded. This was not just a technical matter—the deadlines in foreclosure [including those for reinstating the payments and the right to redeem (save) the home]—run from the date of service of process. Exhibit B is a timeline of the foreclosure process, a piece to which I contributed early on and which has been edited by others as laws and procedures change. Lying about service of process shaves time off the process and deprives the homeowner of rights to which they are entitled under law.

EXHIBIT B

ILLINOIS FORECLOSURE TIMELINE (Illinois Legal Aid Online, www.illinoislegalaid.org, current as of 4/17/2019)

The complaint filed: If you have fallen behind on your mortgage payments, the bank's attorney will start a foreclosure lawsuit in court. They do this by filing a Complaint. After the case is filed, you will start to get a lot of junk mail. Beware of foreclosure rescue scams!

Receive Summons and Complaint: The Sheriff or a process server delivers a copy of the Complaint to you. They also give you a Summons which tells you when and where to come to court. They can also leave these things with a family member who lives with you and who is at least 13 years old.

0-1 months

Response: You have 30 days after you receive the Summons to file an Answer and Appearance, or file a motion. Learn more about responding to a mortgage foreclosure case.

1-2 months

Case management court date: The bank's attorney must go to court to update the judge about the property. If you would like to request mediation, you should attend this court date.

2-3 months

Motion for Judgment of Foreclosure and Sale: Notice of the court date for this motion will be mailed to you at the address you listed on your written Appearance.

3-4 months

A court date for Motion for Judgment of Foreclosure and Sale: You may ask the judge to give you time to respond to the motion. If you are working on a loan modification or other workout with the bank, ask the judge to give you time to negotiate an agreement. If you failed to file your Answer and Appearance on time, you might ask for extra time to file them.

4-6 months

Judgment of Foreclosure: If you do not dispute the facts of the case, the judgment of foreclosure will be entered without a trial. You still have at least 90 days to sell the property or otherwise work it out with the bank. This is your "redemption" period.

7-9 months

Public auction: As soon as the redemption period expires, a public auction of the property can be held. There will not be a court date. If you want more time, you must file a motion before the judicial sale.

8-10 months

Final court date: To finalize the sale, the judge must approve the sale. At the same time, the judge will enter an order of eviction (you will get 30 days to move out). In some cases, you may also have a "special right to redeem" for 30 days. You have only 30 days from the final order to file an appeal.

9-11 months

Eviction: You may file a motion to request an extension. It is best to file your motion before your time to move expires.

◆ ◆ ◆

We began providing thorough answers to advice desk patrons, and, outside of two good foreclosure attorneys in Chicago, were the first to do so. Although rarely done before, we began analyzing the date the homeowner was alleged to have defaulted, the amount claimed due, and other allegations. For example, homeowners were sometimes said to have not carried homeowners' insurance—resulting, in one way or another, in a default. In some cases, the homeowner had evidence to prove the required insurance was in place all along, and even had proof of having sent it repeatedly to the foreclosing lender. We began writing good answers, designed to preserve as many of the homeowners' rights as possible. A sample answer and my guide to writing answers is available at www.kellidudley.com. (These may be dated because the law evolves.)

◆ ◆ ◆

EXHIBIT C

SAMPLE FORECLOSURE ANSWER

(Compare with above IMFL complaint.)

ANSWER, AFFIRMATIVE DEFENSE, AND COUNTERCOMPLAINTS

XX are homeowners who live in the property subject to foreclosure with their family. In 2010, XX took out a loan on their residential home to assist with expenses. Subsequently, X became ill and experienced disability and loss of income as a result. Bank, not a party here, modified the loan several times.

XX now face loss of their home through foreclosure and seek to save it by refinancing the mortgage or taking out a new loan—redeeming the mortgage or following any private workout options available. In addition, they assert defenses and counterclaims.

I. ANSWER

1. XX deny the several allegations in Paragraph 1 and, in the affirmative, state as follows:

 a. The Complaint filed by Plaintiff does not comport with 735 ILCS 5/15-1101 et seq. and is not sufficient to foreclose a "Mortgage, Trust Deed or other conveyance in the nature of a Mortgage."
b. Although Plaintiff claims to be the legal holder of the note and mortgage, as successor in interest to Bank (see Complaint, Caption and Para. 3D), Plaintiff is not a party to the Mortgage. The documents relied upon are a Promissory Note and Mortgage Modification Agreement. The Note is dated 7/31/2014 and lists the lender as "Y Bank, N.A., as successor in interest to Z Bank." Complaint, Group Exhibit B. The Mortgage Modification Agreement is dated July 31, 2014 but was not signed until October 3, 2014. It lists the Lender as "Y BANK, N.A., successor in interest to Z BANK." Complaint, Exhibit A. The 2014 Mortgage Modification Agreement and Note appear to be new loans with a new lender, not, at the time of making, a successor to a prior lender, that should have been subject to new disclosures and documentation. The acquisition of Z Bank by Y Bank was not complete until August 18, 2014. EXHIBIT 1.

 c. There are no Unknown Owners or Nonrecord Claimants not ascertainable with reasonable diligence.

2. XX admit that copies of documents are attached. However, there are two sets of mortgages and notes: a set made with Z Bank beginning in 2000 and modified and extended at various times, and another set made with Plaintiff in 2014. XX deny the legal sufficiency of the documents to support a mortgage foreclosure. In the affirmative, they state that Z Bank is not a party to this litigation, and Plaintiff does not have a legally enforceable mortgage.

3. A. XX admit that the attached 2010 instrument is a Mortgage.

B. XX deny the date of the Mortgage is as stated. A mortgage with Z Bank was made in 2000 and modified in 2010 and 2012 as stated. However, the 2014 "modification" was not a modification, but a new attempt to encumber the subject property with a mortgage with Plaintiff, a new lender.

C. XX admit Z Bank was the original mortgagee. They deny that Plaintiff is Z's successor in interest or otherwise has any interest in the mortgage sought to be foreclosed upon.

D. XX admit the name of the Mortgagor is as shown. However, they deny that any mortgage was effectively made with Plaintiff.

E. XX admit the documents appear to have been recorded as stated.

F. XX admit the documents appear to have been recorded as stated.

G. XX deny that they conveyed a fee simple estate to anyone, or that the Trust company did so on their behalf. At most, a mortgage lien was conveyed. XX admit they hold their property in fee simple; however, they deny this interest is subject to any interest of the Plaintiff.

H. XX admit the original indebtedness was $467,500.00.

I. XX admit that the legal description is as shown.

J. XX deny the amount stated is due. There was no loan to mature. If it did, payments have not been properly applied. Plaintiff claims the loan matured in July 2016 (Complaint, Para. 3J) with a balance of $429,312.65. By Plaintiff's own admission, XX made payments after maturity; however, the payments were never applied—the balance remains at $429,312.65 even though payments are reflected as received. EXHIBIT 2.

K. XX deny the per diem is as stated. In the affirmative, they repeat their allegations in Paragraph J above.

L. XX admit the ownership is as shown.

M. XX deny there are unknown owners or non-record claimants that cannot be ascertained with reasonable diligence.

N. XX deny there is any basis for asserting a personal deficiency against them.

O. XX deny Plaintiff is the holder of the Note secured by the 2014 Mortgage. The 2014 Note purports to be between Plaintiff (as a "successor" to Z Bank) and XX. However, Plaintiff was not a "successor" until August 18, 2014 (EXHIBIT 1), about a month after the note was signed.

P. XX deny there are grounds for Plaintiff to seek inclusion of attorney fees and costs since there is no grounds for a mortgage foreclosure by Plaintiff.

Q. There are no grounds for a shortened period of redemption.

R. There has been no waiver of the right of redemption.

S. There are no grounds for appointment of a receiver.

T. XX do not seek a consent judgment of foreclosure at this time.

U. XX admit Plaintiffs seek to terminate the right to possess the real estate as to the persons listed. They deny there are grounds to do so.

4. XX deny there are any Unknown Owners who cannot be ascertained with reasonable diligence.

5. XX deny there are any Nonrecord Claimants who cannot be ascertained with reasonable diligence.

6. XX deny there are any Unknown Beneficiaries who cannot be ascertained with reasonable diligence.

WHEREFORE, Defendants XX respectfully pray this Honorable Court deny all requested relief.

II. Response to Deemed Allegations

7. Deemed allegations set forth in 735 ILCS 5/15-1504(c) are denied:

(1) on the date indicated the obligor of the indebtedness or other obligations secured by the mortgage was justly indebted in the amount of the indicated original indebtedness to the original mortgagee or payee of the mortgage note.

XX admit they were indebted to the original lender in the sum indicated on the Note. They deny all further allegations.

(2) that the exhibits attached are true and correct copies of the mortgage and note and are incorporated and made a part of the complaint by express reference.

XX admit copies of notes and mortgages are attached but deny Plaintiff's standing as set forth more fully above.

(3) that the mortgagor was at the date indicated an owner of the interest in the real estate described in the complaint and that as of that date made, executed and delivered the mortgage as security for the note or other obligations.

XX admit they are owners (through their trust) and that they signed the 2000 mortgage and note with X Bank; they deny that Plaintiff is the mortgagee.

(4) that the mortgage was recorded in the county in which the mortgaged real estate is located, on the date indicated, in the book and page or as the document number indicated.

XX admit the mortgage was recorded as shown.

(5) that defaults occurred as indicated.

XX deny the defaults occurred as indicated. In the affirmative, they assert the mathematical calculations used by Plaintiff are inaccurate as set forth above in their Answer.

(6) that at the time of the filing of the complaint the persons named as present owners are the owners of the indicated interests in and to the real estate described.

XX admit that they (through their trust) are the owners of the real estate. They deny the Plaintiff owns any interest in or lien upon the real estate. In the affirmative, they state Plaintiff had not merged with Z Bank when 2014 documents were signed listing it as Z Bank's successor in interest.

(7) that the mortgage constitutes a valid, prior and paramount lien upon the indicated interest in the mortgaged real estate, which lien is prior and superior to the right, title, interest, claim or lien of all parties and nonrecord claimants whose interests in the mortgaged real estate are sought to be terminated.

XX admit there is a mortgage lien but deny it belongs to Plaintiff. In the affirmative, they state Plaintiff did not properly make a mortgage with them and documents listing Plaintiff as a successor in interest to Z Bank were dated prior to Plaintiff's merger with Z Bank.

(8) that by reason of the defaults alleged, if the indebtedness has not matured by its terms, the same has become due by the exercise, by the plaintiff or other persons having such power, of a right or power to declare immediately due and payable the whole of all indebtedness secured by the mortgage.

XX deny the default as set forth by Plaintiff.

(9) that all notices of default or election to declare the indebtedness due and payable or other notices required to be given have been duly and properly given.

XX admit various notices have been given. They deny the notices were legally effective.

(10) that any and all periods of grace or other period of time allowed for the performance of the covenants or conditions

claimed to be breached or for the curing of any breaches have expired.

XX deny Plaintiff owns the right to foreclose; therefore, they deny any periods of time have expired.

(11) that the amounts indicated in the statement in the complaint are correctly stated and if such statement indicates any advances made or to be made by the plaintiff or owner of the mortgage indebtedness, that such advances were, in fact, made or will be required to be made, and under and by virtue of the mortgage the same constitute additional indebtedness secured by the mortgage.

XX deny the amounts stated in the mortgage are correct. In the affirmative, they state no default occurred prior to the alleged default date or even prior to the filing of the Complaint.

(12) that, upon confirmation of the sale, the holder of the certificate of sale or deed issued pursuant to that certificate or, if no certificate or deed was issued, the purchaser at the sale will be entitled to full possession of the mortgaged real estate against the parties named in against the parties named in clause (T) of paragraph (3) of subsection (a) of Section 15-1504 or elsewhere to the same effect; the omission of any party indicates that plaintiff will not seek a possessory order in the order confirming sale unless the request is subsequently made under subsection (h) of Section 15-1701 or by separate action under Article 9 of this Code.

XX deny this foreclosure is properly brought. In the affirmative, they state they are the only person entitled to possession in addition to those claiming through their present possessory interest.

WHEREFORE, Defendants XX respectfully pray this Honorable

Court deny all requested relief.

II. AFFIRMATIVE DEFENSE: Plaintiff Lacks Standing to Bring this Mortgage Foreclosure Lawsuit and this Honorable Court Lacks Subject Matter Jurisdiction over the Matter Due to Plaintiff's Lack of Standing

8. Plaintiff filed a Complaint to Foreclose Mortgage naming XX as Defendants.

9. The complaint seeks to foreclose a mortgage on XXs' residential property at Park Street, Heights, Illinois 60400.

10. The mortgage which Plaintiff claims it is entitled to foreclose was given by XX to Z Bank in 2010. Plaintiff claims the mortgage was modified, naming it as "successor in interest" to Z Bank in 2014. However, the Mortgage Modification Agreement and Note executed in 2014 bear dates prior to the merger of Plaintiff and Z Bank. The Mortgage Modification Agreement was executed after the merger but bears an earlier date. The Note bears a date entirely pre-dating the merger.

11. Plaintiff cannot collect a debt it does not own, and this Honorable Court lacks subject matter jurisdiction over this cause of action because Plaintiff has no standing.

WHEREFORE, Defendants XX pray this Honorable Court deny all relief requested by Plaintiff.

III. COUNTERCOMPLAINTS

A. VIOLATION OF RESPA

12. As set forth more fully above, Plaintiff/Counterdefendant Y Bank characterized the loan to XX as modification of an existing mortgage loan even though Y Bank was not, at the date of the mortgage, a "successor in interest" to Z Bank.

13. The Z Bank transaction was, if anything, a new residential mortgage loan.

14. Plaintiff/Counterdefendant Y Bank did not provide any new documents to XX.

15. These omissions constitute a violation of the Real Estate Settlement Procedures
Act of 1974 (RESPA), 12 U.S.C. §2601, et seq.

WHEREFORE, Counterplaintiffs XX pray for an order in their favor and against Plaintiff/Counterdefendant actual damages in the amount of at least $4,500,000.00 and such other relief as this Honorable Court deems just and proper.

B. VIOLATION OF THE TRUTH IN LENDING ACT, 15 U.S.C. §1638(b) and 12 C.F.R. §226.18

16. XX restate and reallege the preceding paragraphs twelve through 15 as if set forth in full herein.

17. TILA, 15 U.S.C. § 1601 et seq. requires certain disclosures, including, but not limited to:
a. Clear, conspicuous, and accurate disclosures of loan terms as set forth in 12 C.F.R. 226.18.
b. Every loan charge must be properly disclosed as part of the "amount financed" or "finance charge." 12 C.F.R. 226.18(b), 12 C.F.R. 226.18(d). In addition, disclosures must be made as to the amount financed, right to disclosure of an itemization of the amount financed, the finance charge expressed as an annual percentage rate, the number and amount of payments, repayment due date the loan, the amount of any late payment penalties, etc.
18. XX did not receive any disclosures.
19. With this pleading, XX elect to rescind the mortgage.

WHEREFORE, XX pray this Honorable Court enter an order in their favor and against Plaintiff/Counterdefendant Y Bank:

a. voiding the mortgage lien;

b. declaring that the mortgage on the subject property is rescinded;

c. entering judgment in an amount to be determined at trial;

d. awarding recoverable costs and attorney's fees; and e. awarding any other relief this Honorable Court finds just and proper in the premises.

Thorough answers like these, which my colleagues and I started developing at the Advice Desk and which I continued evolving on my own, can substantially delay a foreclosure lawsuit without violating any ethical rules. Such an answer forces the plaintiff to prove its case, a matter taken without question (and certainly without vitriol) in every kind of case besides foreclosures.

However, those undermining the desk were not limited to the other side. Many non-profit organizations did not want to work all that hard to defend foreclosures, finding it easier to collect grant money while selling funding sources on the belief that "nothing" can be done to stop foreclosure. Many of these non-profit legal organizations went on the attack.

A colleague at a well-funded non-profit contacted me to say, "You are only offending the judges, lawyers for the banks, and clerks with all these papers."

I had a reply ready. "I do not represent the judges, lawyers for the banks, or clerks."

This was not the Cook County way and did not win me any friends. Fortunately, my boss, Ed, stood by me.

"Kelli, I had a complaint from C & Associates (a foreclosure firm)," he said one day after calling me into his office. "They demanded I fire you."

"Good job!" he concluded.

A Few Foreclosures

Around the time of starting the Desk, I decided that, being a new lawyer, I should take one or two foreclosure defense cases to get a feel for the work before advising litigants. At the Desk, we did not represent individual clients as their lawyers—we helped draft documents and described the process, but people in foreclosure represented themselves.

Telling the receptionists and the Clinic I could take a foreclosure or two opened floodgates. While we had not yet reached Recession-era foreclosure levels, people were desperate for help. My phone rang incessantly, and I was barely able to respond to the calls.

However, I found foreclosures could be defended, and homes could be saved. Below is a case study of my first client at the clinic. Her home was saved after a fifteen-year battle. *The Chicago Tribune* covered the matter with a large spread.

WILMA L.: Preserving a home for her elderly mother

I have no idea how one gets papers from the 1970s, stuffed into an even older valise, on top of more recent papers so that pending foreclosure pleadings and current insurance papers stick to the mildewed bottom. However, that is the package Wilma L, an otherwise elegant woman who owned a stately Victorian in a peaceful neighborhood on Chicago's South Side, brought with her to her first appointment. It was my first client appointment as a real attorney. Telling the receptionists at the South Chicago Legal Clinic that I wanted to try my hand at a "few" foreclosures opened the floodgates, but Wilma was the first client to appear.

Wilma's story was as long and uncertain as foreclosures in Chicago are said to be, but it held up over time. Her troubles began with a foreclosure notice years before we met. At that time, a lawyer "friend" offered to help her avoid foreclosure by having her sign her deed over to him and pay him rent. (The story goes, according to foreclosure scammers, that the foreclosing bank and the judge will never figure out what to do if this kind of title transfer takes place. Of course, the mechanisms for continuing a foreclosure with almost no disruption in such cases are well established, but the scammers' stories and promises are consistently compelling to those facing the loss of their homes.)

The loss of the home would have been doubly tragic. It was filled with treasures like vintage dining sets and cocktail glasses, elegant vintage furniture, and original touches that had lasted the century and more with the house. Most importantly, Wilma's mother lived with her, and Wilma was adamant Momma die in the home. Wilma herself was likely in her 60s (going on 35) at the time, so Momma was not young. She was ill and rarely came down to visit, but knowing she would have to leave the home if it was lost spurred me on.

As time went on, Wilma by hook or by crook (and she doubtlessly had a right hook that could make a crook think twice when justified) got her home back from the first scammer. However, within months, another scam took root. This time, the idea of signing over her title and paying rent did not seem so bad. For one thing, the scammer made his way to Wilma through a trusted friend. In addition, he offered a little up-front cash and a dossier of "saved" properties.

Scammer Two had a unique twist: because judges will fairly quickly restore the rightful owner to title in these schemes, he recruited people—mostly young African-American men with steady jobs and good credit—to be his "mentees." In teaching them the business, he would offload properties like Wilma's onto an unsuspecting young mentee, characterized as an investor. The investor, a second victim, would become frustrated when the homeowner did not pay rent. Though there were thousands of variations, the investor would, under the guiding hand of the "mentor," file an eviction or sell the property to another investor—usually another "mentee." Title quickly became clouded beyond comprehension, causing homeowners to lose hope, to be unable to effectively fight the foreclosure and eviction, to be unable to refinance (because of the clouded title), or to otherwise give up. Many left the homes, and the mentees—falsely promised large profits—were left with unproductive properties that could not be legitimately sold. Many young African-American men lost money, ruined their credit rating, and even faced jail time because of the wranglings of the "investor" "mentors," many of whom were attorneys. (Other targeted groups included people with reliable salaries--I specifically recall a group of public schoolteachers and a group of postal workers. Even within these groups, African-Americans were targeted for the brunt of the scam.)

I filed a quiet title action on Wilma's behalf and succeeded in having her eviction case consolidated with her foreclosure. I filed an answer, affirmative defenses and counterclaims to her foreclosure. Now, a patient and long-suffering Chancery (foreclosure) judge could hear the case. Indeed, he did. The judge got involved in the case, urged the parties toward settlement, and even retained it on his docket when he got a new judicial assignment. After about three years, the investment scammer's mentee relented and executed a quit-claim deed, putting Wilma back in title on her home. Momma got to pass away quietly at home, and her children had a lovely funeral and repast. It was good to know she had not had to face a move as the end of her life approached. However, the bank was determined to collect its due. After I quit working for the Clinic and exited my formal involvement in the case, Wilma received clear title to her home in 2015. Her fight had lasted nearly 15 years, and it drug on for twelve years after I got admitted as an attorney and first became involved.

Wilma remains happily in her home and is as strong, independent, and elegant as ever. Her case was complex. The difference between losing and saving it was a competent, determined foreclosure defense.

Non-litigation alternatives were, and are, valuable. However, as neither the "non-profit" nor private "foreclosure defense" bars recognize to this day, homes can be saved through aggressive litigation as well as through various non-litigation alternatives. And that is what this book is about: why I litigated, how I litigated, and how, in return, a leading (self-described) "public intellectual" in the United States (a former judge on the Seventh Circuit Court of Appeals) eventually came to call me a liar.

I am still here, foreclosures can still be litigated, homes can still be saved. Another foreclosure crisis is coming. If we do not change our treatment of homeowners, greater loss and destruction will result. This is not a lie. It is not an exaggeration. It is a warning.

---

[1] "Patrons" refers to the pro se (or self-represented) litigants to whom the Desk provided brief services, such as legal information, document drafting, and advice.

FORECLOSURES ARE NEITHER INDEFENSIBLE NOR UNAVOIDABLE

"The evil that is in the world almost always comes of ignorance, and good intentions may do as much harm as malevolence if they lack understanding." Albert Camus

Ignorance and Intentions

Most lawyers believe foreclosures are not defensible. Rather than working to save a home, most of those acting in good faith advise clients to sell the home. These lawyers see selling the home and using the cash to pay off the mortgage as one of few options. For clients with good jobs and credit histories, lawyers may suggest refinancing the loans. Very few lawyers sit down to read the foreclosure complaint, listen to the client's side of the story, and work to defend the foreclosure. Clients are usually advised to do one of the following:

(a) pay what the bank claims is owed;

(b) refinance the home;
(c) sell the home (including giving it up in a short sale or deed in lieu transaction); or
(d) declare bankruptcy.

Even when given in good faith, this is poor advice. Many foreclosures can be defended, and the alternatives are imperfect. Selling a home and paying off what the bank says is owed may mean paying unjustified late fees, court costs, and attorney fees. Refinancing may mean incorporating unjustified charges into a new loan. The new loan may be unfair, and the foreclosure will reflect badly in any credit report pulled at that time.

Variants of selling the home include a deed in lieu or short sale. A deed in lieu involves giving the foreclosing bank the property. Many homeowners do not understand that a foreclosure judgement is still eventually entered against them after a deed in lieu. In addition, a personal note may be required at the time of closing. The person gives up their house, but may be responsible to pay money the bank says they owe.

Post-foreclosure debt is big business. Debt pursuant to a judgment collects interest at a rate of 9 percent (735 ILCS 5/2-1303). This rate beats the expected return on about any investments. Foreclosing plaintiffs bundle and sell these debts to various predators. A homeowner may get on his or her feet in a few years and find wages from a new job subject to garnishment to satisfy the original debt and the outrageous interest that has accrued. Creditors can be expected to hold on to the debts and proceed to attach liens to assets, like a new home, after the homeowner recovers from the foreclosure.

Illinois has a law providing there is no liability following a deed in lieu (735 ILCS 5/1-1401); however, the possibilities for bad or deceptive drafting, including simply having the homeowner sign an agreement to continue to be financially liable, abound. Even if a balance is forgiven, the homeowner may be liable for paying income taxes on this forgiven debt.

A short sale is much the same. Most foreclosing lenders are rigorous about making sure the homeowner does not benefit in any way. The homeowner gives up his or her home but does not usually make any money. The lawyers for both sides, realtors, title company, and, of course, the foreclosing lender laugh all the way to the bank—a short trip for some. The short sale does not have the statutory protection against a deficiency afforded by law to a deed in lieu. The homeowner in a short sale relies upon skillful and careful drafting by his or her attorney, and that can be a risky proposition. In addition, taxes may be due for any forgiven amount. Some homeowners have completed short sales only to be forced to sign a note at the closing table assuming the remaining mortgage as a personal debt subject to outrageous interest and terms. Some sign without even understanding what it means.

A few good lawyers and negotiators have been able to make short sale and deed in lieu transactions more attractive for homeowners, even arranging for them to receive financial compensation for walking away form their homes. Largely, these successful negotiators are also skillful and devoted litigators. The banks are not offering money to homeowners as gifts: they are avoiding the costs of litigation, including the possibility the litigator will help the homeowner raise counterclaims or even defeat the foreclosure.

Finally, bankruptcy works for very few—even when they are lucky enough to hire an attorney who is acting in good faith and is competent. Few people understand that a Chapter 13 (for which advertisers bellow, "Keep your house, car, and possessions!") means paying two monthly payments on time, every month. One payment is the regular payment—the one they couldn't make, landing them in this trouble. The other payment is a "catch-up" payment toward their arrears made to the bankruptcy trustee.

If either of these is late (or if the lawyer pockets the money on the way to the bankruptcy trustee's office), the bank will be able to proceed with the foreclosure. A Chapter 7 bankruptcy often means giving up the home, a fact not thoroughly explained to homeowners, in many cases, until the Sheriff is at the door with an eviction order. Even well-intentioned attorneys sometimes make errors, thinking a home will fall within a bankruptcy exemption when it does not. The results for the homeowner are disastrous: loss of the home as well as bankruptcy costs and fees.

There are times when a home cannot be saved. In some cases, homeowners have lived out the usefulness of the home and want to move on. Moving forward without a debt—the "deficiency" judgment that becomes a personal debt if the home is sold at an auction after foreclosure for less than the bank says is owed —is a goal from many. In these cases, Illinois law provides for "consent foreclosure," governed by 735 ILCS 5/15-1402. The legal work involved consists largely of calling opposing counsel, waiting for an answer, and relaying the response. Even though this legal maneuver allows the homeowner to escape future debt, few "defense" lawyers use it. Primarily, this is because it does not result in a large legal bill. Compared to the short sales and deeds-in-lieu discussed above, the consent foreclosure offers little opportunity to bill the client. "Defense" lawyers often favor their pockets over the client's wellbeing. I helped hundreds of people using this method, sometimes charging nothing, often charging $50.00. The most lucrative consent foreclosure I did kept the homeowner in his home without cost to him for eight months and allowed him to leave when he retired from his job without fear of debt. The homeowner paid me $250.00 and took me out to dinner on his way out of town. At that time, he returned the key to the home to me, concerned the foreclosing lender not damage the home by breaking in. (Many homeowners share this touching concern for the preservation of their home and community. In every case where homeowners have taken the time to coordinate return of the key to my opposing counsel, the bank has hired inept contractors to secure the home. Whether for fun or to add to their profit, the contractors invariably break in to the home and "secure" it in a way to create an eyesore for the community.)

Foreclosure Defenses

Even though "no defense to foreclosure" remains the rallying cry of incompetent or inexperienced counsel, foreclosures are neither inevitable nor indefensible.
In fact, there are real defenses to foreclosure.

As discussed above, early in the foreclosure crisis, banks did not attach the mortgage and note to the complaint. This is required by the IMFL [see sample foreclosure complaint; 735 ILCS 5/15-1504(a)(1)]. The first two allegations of the complaint usually include that the mortgage and note are attached as exhibits A and B. In addition to the IMFL, a party suing to enforce a contract in Illinois in state court has to either attach the contract or recite the relevant portions in the complaint. 735 ILCS 5/2-606. These early, no-attachment complaints were susceptible to dismissal, and judges routinely granted motions to dismiss on this basis.

In addition, service on homeowners is often "sewer" service. Service is the process required by the Constituion to let a defendant know about a lawsuit and to give him or her notice of the allegations and an opportunity to be heard. This is usually achieved by delivering a copy of the complaint and a summons to the homeowner.

EXHIBIT D is a sample summons consisting of five pages:

2120 - Served   2121 - Served
2220 - Not Served   2221 - Not Served
2320 - Served By Mail   2321 - Served By Mail
2420 - Served By Publication   2421 - Served By Publication
☐ Summons ☐ Alias Summons   (07/25/18) CCCH 0100 A

IN THE CIRCUIT COURT OF COOK COUNTY, ILLINOIS
COUNTY DEPARTMENT - CHANCERY DIVISION

No: _____

_____

v.

Case Management Date: _____

Time: _____ ○ AM ○ PM

Courtroom: _____

MORTGAGE FORECLOSURE SUMMONS

To each Defendant:

YOU ARE SUMMONED and required to file an appearance, pay the required fee (unless the Court determines you cannot afford to pay this fee), and answer or otherwise plead in response to the attached Complaint within 30 days. A copy of the Complaint is attached to this Summons. To file your appearance and pleadings you need access to the internet and a credit card for payment. Please visit www.cookcountyclerkofcourt.org to initiate this process. Kiosks with internet access are available at all Clerk's Office locations. Please refer to the last page of this document for location information.

> YOU MAY STILL BE ABLE TO SAVE YOUR HOME.
> DO NOT IGNORE THIS DOCUMENT.
> GO TO PAGE 2 OF THIS SUMMONS FOR INFORMATION ON FREE HELP FROM THE COURT.

You must file within 30 days after service of this summons, not counting the day of service.

If you fail to do so, a judgment by default may be entered against you for the relief requested in the complaint.

To the Officer:

This summons must be returned by the officer or other person to whom it was given for service, with endorsement of service and fees, if any, immediately after service. If service cannot be made, this summons shall be returned so endorsed. This summons may not be served later than 30 days after its date.

This is an attempt to collect a debt and any information obtained will be used for that purpose.

Dorothy Brown, Clerk of the Circuit Court of Cook County, Illinois
cookcountyclerkofcourt.org
Page 1 of 6

Mortgage Foreclosure Summons   (07/25/18) CCCH 0100 B

E-filing is now mandatory for documents in civil cases with limited exemptions. To e-file, you must first create an account with an e-filing service provider. Visit http://efile. illinoiscourts.gov/service-providers.htm to learn more and to select a service provider. If you need additional help or have trouble e-filing, visit http://www.illinoiscourts.gov/FAQ/ gethelp.asp, or talk with your local circuit clerk's office.

Atty. No.: _____   Witness,

Atty Name: _____   _____

Atty. for: _____   Clerk of the Court

Address: _____   Date of Service: _____
                                       (To be inserted by officer on copy left with de-
City: _____   fendant or other person)

State: ____ Zip: _____

Telephone: _____

Primary Email: _____

Mortgage Foreclosure Summons   **(07/25/18) CCCH 0100 C**

IMPORTANT INFORMATION FOR HOMEOWNERS IN FORECLOSURE
HOW TO SAVE YOUR PROPERTY - PLEASE READ - DO NOT IGNORE

1. POSSESSION: The lawful occupants of a home have the right to live in the home until a judge enters an order for possession. In most cases, if you continue to live in your home, you will have at least nine (9) months before you have to move.

2. OWNERSHIP: You continue to own your home until the court rules otherwise.

---

3. WORKOUT OPTIONS: The mortgage company does not want to foreclose on your home if there is any way to avoid it. Call your mortgage company:

                          (Homeowner's current mortgage service)

or its attorneys to find out the alternatives to foreclosure. To get help filing an Appearance and Answer, contact the Chancery Division Advice Desk, Room CL-16 of the Richard J. Daley Center, 50 W. Washington St., Chicago, IL 60602, Monday through Friday, 8:30 am to 3:00 pm. THESE SERVICES ARE FREE.

---

4. LAWYER: If you do not have a lawyer, you may contact CARPLS Legal Aid Hotline at (312) 738-9200 for legal advice or visit the Advice Desk (see above). You may also call Chicago Volunteer Legal Services at (312) 332-1624 or the Legal Assistance Foundation of Metropolitan Chicago at (312) 341-1070.

5. REINSTATEMENT: As the homeowner you have the right to bring the mortgage current (that means paying all late payments, penalties, fees and costs) within 90 days after you receive the summons.

6. REDEMPTION: As the homeowner you have the right to sell your home, refinance, or pay off the loan during the redemption period, which is at least seven (7) months after you receive the summons.

7. PAYOFF AMOUNT: You have the right to obtain a written statement of the amount necessary to pay off your loan. Your mortgage company (identified in #3 above) must provide you this statement within 10 business days of receiving your request, provided that your request is in writing and includes your name, the address of the property, and the mortgage account or loan number. Your first payoff statement will be free.

8. SURPLUS: As the homeowner you have the right to petition the court for any excess money (i.e., if your home is sold for more than you owe) that results from a foreclosure sale of your home. In many cases you do not need a lawyer to do this. The Chancery Division Advice Desk, Room CL-16 of the Richard J. Daley Center, will assist you in preparing all the necessary papers at no charge. The Advice Desk is open Monday through Friday, 8:30 am to 3:00 pm.

9. GET ADVICE: This information does not replace the advice of a professional. You may have other options. Get professional advice from a lawyer or HUD-certified housing counselor about your rights and options to avoid foreclosure.

---

10. PROCEED WITH CAUTION: YOU MAY BE CONTACTED BY PEOPLE OFFERING TO HELP YOU AVOID FORECLOSURE. BEFORE ENTERING INTO ANY TRANSACTION WITH PEOPLE OFFERING TO HELP YOU, PLEASE CONTACT A LAWYER, GOVERNMENT OFFICIAL, OR HUD-CERTIFIED HOUSING COUNSELOR FOR ADVICE.

Dorothy Brown, Clerk of the Circuit Court of Cook County, Illinois
cookcountyclerkofcourt.org
Page 3 of 6

Mortgage Foreclosure Summons   (07/25/18) CCCH 0100 D

INFORMACION IMPORTANTE PARA PROPIETARIOS DE CASA EN PROCESO DE EJECUCION HIPOTECARIA:
COMO SALVAR SU CASA – POR FAVOR LEA ESTO – NO LO IGNORE -USTED HA RECIBO UN DOCUMENTO LEGAL PORQUE HA SIDO DEMANDADO POR SU BANCO HIPOTECARIO

1. POSESION: Los ocupantes legítimos de la vivienda tienen el derecho de vivir en la casa hasta que el juez emita, por escrito, una Orden de Posesión judicial. En la mayoría de los casos, si continúa viviendo en su casa, tendrá por lo menos nueve (9) meses antes que tenga que mudarse.

2. TITULARIDAD: Usted sigue siendo propietario de su casa hasta que el juez emita una decisión contraria.

3. OPCIONES DE NEGOCIACION: El prestamista hipotecario no quiere ejecutar sobre su casa si hay alguna manera de evitarlo. Llame a su prestamista hipotecario:

   _____
   (Subraye el nombre del actual prestamista hipotecaria)
   o a sus abogados para averiguar las alternativas a la ejecución hipotecaria. Para obtener ayuda en archivar su Comparecencia en Juicio o Contestación a la Demanda, acuda a la Mesa de Consejo de la División de Chancery, Cuarto CL-16 del Centro Daley, 50 W. Washington St., Chicago, IL 60602, Lunes a Viernes de 8:30 am a 3:00 pm. ESTOS SERVICIOS SON GRATUITOS.

4. ABOGADO: Si no tiene un abogado, puede llamar a la línea gratuita de CARPLS al (312) 738-9200 para asesoría legal y referencias o visite la Mesa de Consejo (véase arriba). O también puede comunicarse con el "Chicago Volunteer Legal Services" al (312) 332-1624 o con el "Legal Assistance Foundation of Metropolitan Chicago" al (312) 341-1070.

5. RESTABLECIMIENTO: Como el propietario usted tiene el derecho de poner al corriente su hipoteca (pagando los pagos retrasados, penalidades, honorarios y costos) dentro de 90 días después de que usted reciba este Emplazamiento.

6. REDENCION DE LA PROPIEDAD: Como el propietario usted tiene el derecho de vender su casa, refinanciar, o pagar el total del préstamo durante el período de redención, que es por lo menos siete (7) meses después que reciba este Emplazamiento.

7. CANTIDAD DEL SALDO: Tiene el derecho de obtener una declaración por escrito de la cantidad necesaria para pagar su préstamo. Su prestamista hipotecario (identificado en el #3 arriba) debe proporcionarle esta declaración dentro de 10 días laborales posteriores a haber recibido su petición, con tal de que su petición sea por escrito e incluya su nombre, dirección de la propiedad y cuenta hipotecaria o número de préstamo. Su primera declaración del saldo será gratis.

8. EXCESO DE BIENES: Como el propietario usted tiene el derecho de solicitarle al tribunal el exceso de dinero (si su casa se vende por mas de lo que debe) que resulte de la venta de ejecución de su casa. En la mayoría de los casos no necesita un abogado para hacerlo. La Mesa de Consejo de la División de Chancery, Cuarto CL-16 del Centro Richard J. Daley, le ayudara a preparar todos los documentos necesarios gratis. El horario de la Mesa de Consejo es de Lunes a Viernes de 8:30 am a 3:00 pm.

Dorothy Brown, Clerk of the Circuit Court of Cook County, Illinois
cookcountyclerkofcourt.org

9. OBTENGA ASESORIA: Esta información no reemplaza asesoría legal de un profesional. Podría tener otras opciones. Obtenga asesoría profesional de un abogado o de un consejero de vivienda certificado por HUD sobre sus derechos y opciones para evitar la ejecución hipotecaria.

10. PROCEDA CON PRECAUCION: USTED PODRA SER CONTACTADO POR GENTE OFRECIENDOLE AYUDA PARA EVITAR LA EJECUCION HIPOTECARIA. ANTES DE REALIZAR CUALQUIER TRAMITE CON PERSONAS OFRECIENDOLE AYUDA, POR FAVOR COMUNIQUESE CON UN ABOGADO, REPRESENTANTE GUBERNAMENTAL O CONSEJERO DE VIVIENDA CERTIFICADO POR HUD PARA ASESORIA.

In Illinois, the summons and complaint can be given to the homeowner or left at his or her residence with a member of the household who is over age 13 and able to understand the nature of the papers (735 ILCS 5/2-201). Leaving the papers stuck on the door or in the mailbox, commonly used methods, are not legally allowed. Historically, after a Sheriff could not serve the home-owner, the bank would have a "special process server" appointed. The process server was employed at the whim of the plaintiff's at-torneys, and usually only got paid if service was made—if a copy of the summons and complaint was properly served on the home-owner. Eager to please the corporate overlords, the special pro-cess servers eagerly threw summonses away or served them in-correctly, then provided false affidavits swearing, under oath, proper service was achieved. Homeowners complaining of bad service were often successful in having it quashed (set aside). One homeowner said the summons was not put in his hands but left on his porch. When he brought me the paperwork, the leaves and debris stuck to the paper supported his story. Often, people with androgynous names were said to have been served and the gender would be listed incorrectly. A petite, blond female "Kelly" would show up where the return of service described Ving Rhames, the process server's stereotype of a person in foreclosure [or maybe just the reflection of the probability that those facing foreclosure would be black, given that African-Americans were 33 percent more likely to get subprime loans in the first place (Ira Goldstein & Dan Urevick-Ackelsberg. *Subprime Lending, Mortgage Foreclosures and Race: how far have we come and how far do we have to go?* available at http://kirwaninstitute.osu.edu/docs/pdfs/goldstein_trf_paper.pdf, last accessed 10/24/2019). In one par-ticularly fun showdown early in my career, a special process ser-ver swore he served my client's 20-year-old son at home. He stuck by his assertion, right up until I produced documents showing the young man was in college in Georgia, marked present in class and using his credit cards around Atlanta that day. Many plain-tiff's lawyers simply did not understand the rules of service at all. The same lawyer who was my opposing counsel in the case in-volving the student away at school when served in Chicago be-came a friend. A few weeks after our hearing (where I won), she ranted about a colleague who contested service "on a neighbor." In Illinois, there is absolutely no support for the idea service of process can be made upon one's neighbor; it can only be made upon the person or a member of their household. There is no Ned Flanders (neighbor) exception. Okaley dokely?

Objecting to service of process must be done at the beginning of a case, before the merits (like whether a payment was actually missed) are discussed. Many homeowners inadvertently give up this important right by being tricked into going to court when they receive inadequate service of process. It is quite natural to say, "But I didn't default!" This innocent assertion goes to the merits and may be held to waive the right to contest service of process. As if that is not enough, the Illinois legislature, always eager to accommodate banking industry campaign donors, has amended the IMFL to limit the time for objecting to jurisdiction to 60 days (735 ILCS 5/15-1505.6). It is unclear how a court, without jurisdiction, can determine the 60 days have elapsed and subject the homeowner to jurisdiction. To do so is in direct contravention of Constitutional guarantees. In addition, the Circuit Court of Cook County adopted an order allowing foreclosure plaintiffs—and no one else—to skip the legally-mandated step of placing summonses with the Cook County Sheriff for service and go directly to a special process server (Cook County General Administrative Order 2007-03). The First District Appellate Court affirmed this in *U.S. Bank v. Dzis*, 2011 IL App (1st) 102812. To further paraphrase Ned Flanders, "I've done everything the Constitution says—even the stuff that contradicts the other stuff!"

The service of process requirement is not a mere procedural step. It is guaranteed by the Constitution. In practical terms, many of the rights homeowners have to resolve a foreclosure by paying off the home or paying the amount the plaintiff claims is due are time limited. The time begins at the moment the homeowner is served. If this time is improperly calculated from January when the homeowner is not served until July, for example, trims the time to gather needed money for financing by six months.

Substantive Defenses to Foreclosure

Substantive defenses to foreclosure also exist. To raise these defenses, lawyers must carefully read the complaint, research public records, and consult with the client. Math may be required. Sometimes, the wrong property is listed in the complaint. I have had several cases where the mortgage was not recorded against all the parcels involved in the foreclosure. No mortgage means no lien means no foreclosure. A particularly nefarious foreclosure upon the wrong property is Exhibit E:

Case: 1:02-cv-06024 Document #: 72 Filed: 05/11/04 Page 2 of 2 PageID #:311
(Reserved for use by the Court)

ORDER

Fisher and Fisher has moved that this court reconsider, alter, or amend its order imposing sanctions. In a submission filed pursuant to the order of this court, Fisher and Fisher have withdrawn certain of the requests made in its motion. Specifically: "Fisher & Fisher withdraws its request that the Court reconsider the provisions of the March 17, 2004 Order which require all current Fisher & Fisher attorneys and future attorneys employed by Fisher & Fisher during the next two years to attend a sixteen (16) hour course on topics relating to federal subject matter jurisdiction." And: "Fisher & Fisher also withdraws its request that the Court reconsider the requirement of a sixteen (16) hour course." The portion of the motion to reconsider that has not been withdrawn is encapsulated in another statement contained in Fisher and Fisher's submission:

Fisher & Fisher reiterates its assertion that, although mistakes were admittedly made in connection with the underlying litigation, there was no unreasonable or vexatious conduct. Fisher & Fisher does not waive its assertion that no sanctions were warranted.

Fisher and Fisher continues to neither accept responsibility nor show any remorse for its conduct in this case. To reiterate the basic facts: Fisher and Fisher had its process server attempt personal service on the late Mattie Sullivan-Moore at an incorrect address; she was not present at that address, so based on that attempted service Fisher and Fisher was permitted to serve by publication; a default judgment in favor of plaintiff was entered; and a special commissioner sold the property. If this were all that had happened, the court might well agree with Fisher and Fisher's assertion that "although mistakes were admittedly made . . . there was no unreasonable or vexatious conduct."

This, however, was far from all that occurred. After the judgment and sale, Fisher and Fisher learned that the address that it had been using throughout the proceedings was incorrect. This of course meant that the attempt at personal service was not sufficient to warrant service by publication. At this point, a reasonably competent second year law student would have realized that it was necessary to move to vacate the sale and judgment, and then to start over with proper service of process. Instead, Fisher and Fisher made a motion to correct scrivener's error, as if a failure to serve defendant with process could be corrected by correcting the address on the documents filed with the court. This egregious, unreasonable, and, yes, vexatious conduct resulted in the late Mattie Sullivan-Moore being evicted without ever having been served with process, and so without having been given the notice and opportunity to be heard required by due process. Nowhere in the motion to reconsider does Fisher and Fisher address itself to this fundamental, egregious misconduct.

The attorney who came to court moving for a renewed order of possession aggravated the situation. It will not do to say that he was unaware of the failure to make proper service because he "was handling the matter as a separate eviction proceeding." The sanction in this case was imposed against the law firm, and other attorneys in the firm were in possession of that knowledge, paradoxically whether they realized it or not. The failure of the law firm to have in place a mechanism whereby important information about the foreclosure proceedings was in the possession of the attorney handling the eviction is not mitigating, but rather an aspect of the improper conduct in this case. Moreover, his attempt to keep Ms. Sullivan-Moore's daughter from assisting her in addressing the court while Ms. Sullivan-Moore was attempting with difficulty to approach the lectern using her walker, is found by the court to have been an attempt by Fisher and Fisher to deny Ms. Sullivan-Moore an opportunity to tell the court about the serious injustice that had been done to her. In the context in which it occurred, with Ms. Sullivan-Moore present (and therefore available for confirmation of anything her daughter said) and obviously greatly incapacitated (she died less than two months after the hearing in question), her daughter's attempt to assist could not reasonably be viewed as an improper attempt by a non-attorney to represent her.

Fisher and Fisher complains about this court's statement that "Fisher & Fisher's unreasonable and vexatious actions imposed substantial burdens and stress upon on [sic] the late Ms Sullivan-Moore, stress which may possibly have hastened her demise." The court stands by this statement. Being improperly evicted and having to come to court to keep from being wrongfully evicted again was certainly stressful and burdensome. It is certainly possible this stress may have hastened her demise, particularly in view of her certificate of death indicating the cause of her death as coronary artery disease. In view of the requests of the motion withdrawn in the submission, the court does not believe it is necessary to enumerate the facts underlying its conclusion that there was a larger pattern of violations of the rules of federal civil procedure by the attorneys of Fisher and Fisher.

Therefore, the motion to reconsider is being denied.

In this case, the wrong property was taken in foreclosure and the elderly homeowner, whose home was not subject to the mortgage the bank sought to foreclose upon, was wrongfully evicted. The homeowner passed away before the matter was resolved, but the law firm was ordered to attend classes on civil procedure and pay the woman's estate a modest sum. Rather than attend the requisite classes and pay the monies as ordered, the firm in question in the case went out of business and merged with another firm, escaping liability, after the Seventh Circuit Court of Appeals affirmed the sanctions order [*U.S. Bank National Association, N.D. v. Sullivan-Moore*, 406 F.3d 465 (7th Cir. 2005)]. They continued to do business under the new name without paying any price for their misconduct. A similar tactic was used by a firm that admitted it (through "young associates") altered affidavits of debt signed by its bank clients after they were signed. While thousands of foreclosures had to be vacated, the judgments were summarily entered again in almost every case. The firm faced no significant liability. Plaintiffs' firms routinely use corporate structure and name changes to avoid ever having to pay more than the mildest *mea culpa* for malfeasance.

In other cases, the mortgage amount is calculated incorrectly, either because of fuzzy math or because the bank wrongfully induced the homeowner to send money each month and then failed to credit the account, continuing with the foreclosure. I have had several cases where the banks, eager to foreclose, alleged a default. Taking their allegations of sums paid and when the default occurred, the homeowner was not behind but ahead by several months. In other cases, the banks accepted—but did not credit—as much as $65,000, then declared a default. In many cases, the uncredited amounts were regular monthly payments. In other cases, they were new payments that were the result of a purported "modification" of the loan. Math scares people. Understandably, most self-represented people assume the bank's math is correct. Inexcusably, many foreclosure "defense" attorneys neglect checking this important fact. If called upon to justify their figures in court, most foreclosing plaintiffs and their attorneys cannot or will not do so. This includes both attorney fees and costs and the actual alleged amount due under the original mortgage.

In many cases, banks fail to properly exchange and record documents related to which entity had the right to collect a loan. Were I to borrow $5.00 for lunch, you might sell the right to collect the $5.00 back from me to Joe. Because you figured it was risky to lend to me, you would decide $4.00 payable now, from Joe, was a surer bet than collecting the entire $5.00 from me. Joe would pay you $4.00 for the right to collect and would make a $1.00 profit if he succeeded in collecting the full $5.00 from me. However, I would object to paying Joe without proof you sold the loan to him. After all, I could easily pay Joe $5.00 Tuesday and then find you on my doorstop—disclaiming all knowledge of Joe —on Wednesday. In that case, I might well end up repaying my loan twice.

Naturally, homeowners are stunned when banks transfer their loans, often without even the bare minimum of notice mandated by law. Some quit paying when they don't recognize the statement from Bank X because they only borrowed from Bank Y. Other homeowners cannot obtain documentation to support the amount the foreclosing bank claims due.

Defenses based on improperly documented loan transfers gained traction until they were abused by "save your home" attorneys who took large sums of money and did little or no work. Many would file a Motion to Dismiss based on lack of standing (errors in the paperwork when the loan changed hands) even if there was no basis for it in the individual homeowner's file. Understandably, judges became frustrated at this abuse of process, and the First District Court eventually issued a decision striking down "show me the note" defenses in most cases, *Mers v. Barnes*, 406 Ill.App. 3d 1 (1st Dist. 2010). The real issue in *Mers v. Barnes* was that a defendant, who had hired an attorney, did not file an answer or response to the foreclosure on time. After judgement allowing the bank to sell the home at auction was entered, the attorney moved to vacate (cancel) the judgement. Illinois has two code sections allowing judgements to be vacated. The motion to vacate permitted by the first code section, 735 ILCS 5/2-1301, must be brought within 30 days of the judgement. The other, 735 ILCS 5/2-1401, provides that a party can file a motion to vacate after 30 days from the judgement date but within two years. In this case, the defense attorney filed a motion to vacate under Section 1401 within 30 days. The judge struck the motion as untimely —it should have been filed as a motion to vacate under Section 1301 (within 30 days). However, by the time the attorney refiled the motion under Section 1301, more than 30 days had elapsed. By then, the proper motion to file was one under Section 1401. This led to denial of the motion and an appeal that resulted in a decision that closed off a major avenue for homeowners seeking to defend foreclosures.

Good defenses sometimes are available to assist homeowners. However, haphazard application and form pleadings by "save your home" lawyers have caused courts to, understandably, view almost every defense with skepticism.

"DEADBEATS": THEY DON'T MATTER ANYWAY

*"*T*he man from the country has not expected such difficulties: the law should always be accessible for everyone, he thinks ... ". Franz Kafka*

Inherent in lawyers' refusal to try to defend foreclosure cases are deep-seated prejudices against homeowners who fall into foreclosure. It is easy for lawyers to ignore the needs of those whose woes seem to be partially brought on by poor choices or bad behavior. Like most consumers, homeowners sometimes make bad budgeting choices. But the mortgage foreclosure crisis disproportionately impacted communities of color, and racism and classism likely contribute to the misconception homeowners are to blame for poor daily financial decisions. Many of those living in poverty take calculated risks (*e.g.*, allowing a utility bill to fall into arrears during the winter shut-off moratorium) because they live on a fixed income and cannot afford basic necessities otherwise. Some lawyers may also focus on the fact clients contribute to their problems by choosing homes driven by vanity (and the homeowners' own racism). Even those driven into debt by medical bills or job loss beyond their control easily share some culpability by choosing a high-priced home that requires a large mortgage rather than finding a less expensive one based on a need for shelter. Working people are not immune from the tendency of wealthier people to give into silly notions that some neighborhoods are "safer" and more worthy than others (those who stay in the old neighborhood be damned) or that a two-car garage (soon to be overflowing with junk and unavailable for parking anyway) is nirvana.

A friend of mine who is an ethical and competent bankruptcy attorney shared with me several years ago that he had never filed a bankruptcy petition that did not include a cable bill. In other words, people facing large, unmanageable debts chose to pay for mind-rotting junk to flow into their homes rather than reserving the money for necessities. Similarly, most clients I have had have outspent me on everything from clothes to car. Perhaps the most spectacular example was a client who had never been current from the inception on three mortgages used to buy a $300,000 home on a $50,000 per year salary. At least one mortgage was obtained through lying. The client quit paying me about a quarter into his case, redirecting his money to a large truck. He was "too embarrassed" to drive the car he already had to work (but it was okay for his lawyer to wonder if her used Hyundai would make it to court in his remote rural county). This is the only client who ever listed me on bankruptcy discharge papers! Suffice it to say, there are many, many people who have expected me to do without their agreed-upon payment so they could live high on the hog. It always baffles me a little as to how someone could be so callous as to expect unpaid labor—along with out-of-pocket expenses like copies, mailing, gas, and parking—to support an extravagant lifestyle. The psychopathology involved is almost as stunning as the irrationality—alienating the person who is working to save your home and your "baller" lifestyle is just not smart.

Simply put, there are lots of reasons lawyers may not feel sympathy for many of those in foreclosure. Regardless of where the blame lies, homeowners in foreclosure are entitled to a competent defense. At minimum, they are entitled to receive the services for which they contract and pay. Those contacting legal aid resources are entitled to accurate information, including a disclaimer or a suggestion the homeowner seek further advice where the organization is constrained by financial or ideological considerations.

Given the above, it makes sense for some attorneys to turn away clients or to withdraw from cases after representation agreements are not honored. After all, no one is expected to work for free. Even an attorney who is performing *pro bono* work and being paid by a non-profit organization has a right to insist rules be followed (truthfulness, providing documents on request, paying out-of-pocket costs if agreed, etc.). What is stunning, however, is the number of lawyers willing to take advantage of clients—taking large sums of money and then failing to help. In some cases, it appears nothing can be done to help the client, but the lawyer accepts money on a blatantly false promise to "save your home."

Turning a client away is one thing; actively putting them in a worse position just to receive an unearned legal fee is another. However, it is more often than not that foreclosure "defense" attorneys put the client in a worse position than if the client did not hire any lawyer at all. At very least, a client who loses a home but has some savings can obtain substitute housing. If that same client hires a lawyer who makes no real effort to save the home (or, worse, files paperwork that hastens the loss of the home), then the client ends up broke—having spent money on legal fees for illusory service—and more likely to be homeless. In addition, the client may face misinformation from the foreclosure "defense" lawyer. For example, the lawyer may lie about the likely date of an eviction, causing the homeowner to be caught unawares. When one is unable to plan when to move to avoid eviction, personal belongings may be stolen or ruined by the elements as the homeowner seeks the means to move.

Race

The failure to help those in foreclosure, the erection of systemic barriers to effective help, and the willingness to steal from those in foreclosure—taking money under a false pretense that a foreclosure "defense" will be tendered (and doing so with impunity) —is not primarily rooted in the behavior of foreclosure defendants. It is largely rooted in their identity, as yet another way of decimating the black middle class. While the prevalence of subprime loans to African-Americans is fairly widely recognized (Ira Goldstein & Dan Urevick-Ackelsberg. *Subprime Lending, Mortgage Foreclosures and Race: How far have we come and how far do whave to go?*), courts are all too willing to gloss over the racial ramifications of predatory behavior toward foreclosure defendants by the foreclosure "defense" bar.

Those who preyed on homeowners did so based upon factors protected by the Fair Housing Act (FHA). Examples include race, ethnicity, national origin, and religion.

The African-American community was hardest hit by foreclosure rescue "defense" attorneys. Several advertised aggressively on billboards in black communities and on radio stations serving the black community. One hosted an "informational" radio show (having purchased advertising in large chunks of time) on WVON. Not only did WVON's advertising rate sheet show a 95 percent black listening audience, the call letters originally stood for "Voice of the Negro" when it was established in 1963 to empower black people. It now has changed to "Voice of the Nation" per its website.

I represented a homeowner victim of a foreclosure "defense" attorney who advertised through a "radio show" as well as aggressive billboard campaigns in African-American neighborhoods. It was a lengthy battle. The attorney, defendant in our FHA case, tried to stymie my client's FHA case by getting a restraining order to prevent me from talking to my client for nearly 16 months. The Order was so broad it seemed to prohibit me from talking to virtually anyone about the FHA:

Kelli Dudley

Order   (2/24/05) CCG N002

IN THE CIRCUIT COURT OF COOK COUNTY, ILLINOIS

Ernest Fenton, Et al

v.   No. _2013 L 0 CCC4___

Kelli Dudley, Et al

ORDER page 2 of 3

2) That the Defendants cease to contact any former or current client and/or employer of the Law Office of Ernest E. Fenton;

3) That the Defendants cease to attempt to take Plaintiff's client away from Plaintiff's already-established law practice including, but not limited to clients obtained by the Law Office of Ernest E. Fenton from community, organizations, churches, or non-profit entities

4) That Defendants cease to make false and defamatory remarks regarding: a. Plaintiff's retainer agreement or any related funding issue between the Law Office of Ernest E. Fenton and clients; b. Misleading and false statements about Plaintiff, the attorney, of the Law Office of Ernest E. Fenton, or the staff

Atty. No.: _06189___

Name: _The Law Office of Ernest E. Fenton_ ENTERED:

Atty. for: _Plaintiff_

Address: _995 W. 175th Street, Suite 1 East_

City/State/Zip: _Homewood, IL 60430_ Dated: _____

       Judge Loretta Eadie-Daniels

Telephone: _708-001-7264_ Judge JUL 17 2013 Judge's No.

       Circuit Court 1813

DOROTHY BROWN, CLERK OF THE CIRCUIT COURT OF COOK COUNTY, ILLINOIS

Copy Distribution - White: 1. ORIGINAL - COURT FILE Canary: 2. COPY Pink: 3. COPY

From the get-go, the Order was illegal, entered by a state court while the case was pending in front of a Federal court. Situations like this, where the case is removed to Federal court, result in a "stay" of the state court case. The state court is supposed to refrain from doing anything until the Federal court is done with its action. Of course, state court judges count on lawyers to be candid with them about matters. In an action one judge later characterized as "dumb and dumber," the attorneys wrote to me acknowledging the case was stayed, but stating they would go forward anyway. They were eventually sanctioned. Two attorneys were ordered to pay me money, and the Illinois rules governing attorneys require attorneys to comply with court orders. Mr. Snyder promptly paid; Mr. Fenton has not paid as mandated by the judge's order, which follows:

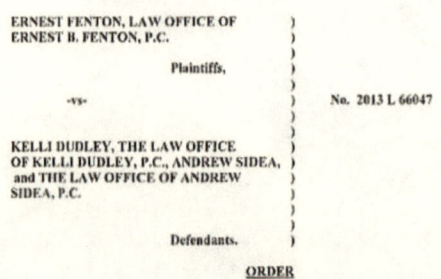

IN THE CIRCUIT COURT OF COOK COUNTY, ILLINOIS
COUNTY DEPARTMENT – LAW DIVISION

ERNEST FENTON, LAW OFFICE OF)
ERNEST B. FENTON, P.C.)
)
           Plaintiffs,)
)
-vs-   )   No. 2013 L 66047
)
)
KELLI DUDLEY, THE LAW OFFICE)
OF KELLI DUDLEY, P.C., ANDREW SIDEA,)
 and THE LAW OFFICE OF ANDREW)
SIDEA, P.C.   )
)
          Defendants.)

ORDER

This cause coming to be heard on the motion of the defendant Kelli Dudley seeking sanctions against the plaintiffs and attorney Brian G. Snyder pursuant to Illinois Supreme Court Rule 137. The parties having been provided with the opportunity to address this motion and arguments having been made on the behalf of all involved, the following background is provided and the ensuing Order is hereby entered sanctioning Ernest Fenton and Brian G. Snyder.

This above captioned matter centers around a complaint filed by the plaintiffs (hereinafter referred to as "Fenton") against the defendants (hereinafter referred to as ("Dudley") and alleging numerous counts including Conversion, Tortious Interference with Business Relations and Defamation (Slander.)

Background

The defendants were retained to represent a homeowner in a lawsuit that dealt with the rendering of legal services to Ms. Davis by Fenton and involving the Fair Housing Act, 42 U.S.C. § 3601et seq. and the Civil Rights

1

Act of 1866, 42 U.S.C. § 3601.   That matter was filed in federal court in the Northern District of Illinois, Eastern Division, and was captioned as *Tonya Davis v. Ernest B, Fenton, Law Offices of Ernest B. Fenton, P.C. and Legal Services, Inc.* No. 13 cv 03224.

Subsequent to the filing of the federal matter on July 3, 2013, the plaintiffs filed the instant matter in the Circuit Court of Cook County, Illinois seeking damages and injunctive relief based on allegations the defendants had damaged the plaintiffs by unlawfully accessing and using privileged information, as well as making slanderous statements that caused damage to their reputations and resulted in a loss of business.

On July 14, 2013, the defendant, Kelli Dudley, sought to remove the instant matter to federal court and filed a Notice of Removal in United States District Court for the Northern District of Illinois, Eastern Division. She also filed a Notice of Filing of Notice of Removal with the Clerk of the Circuit Court of Cook County Illinois and served (U.S.mail) a copy to: *The Law Office of Ernest B. Fenton* on July 15, 2013.

On July 16, 2013, a string of emails concerning a Motion for a Preliminary Injunction were exchanged between Dudley and Brian G. Snyder. The initial email from Snyder to Dudley was sent as a reminder to Dudley of the Motion being set to be heard the next day at 9:00 a.m. in room 207 of the Markham courthouse. Dudley replied with an admonition that the order would be void and that she would seek sanctions against him. Snyder then followed up with another email informing Dudley that his office would inform the Judge of the Notice of Removal, that the motion would be pursued and that they would leave it up the judge to decide whether he wants to honor the Notice of Removal.

2

Kelli Dudley

Assocs. v. Kitzman, 307 Ill. App. 3d 92, 240 Ill. Dec. 235, 716 N.E.2d 829,
1999 Ill. App. LEXIS 610 (1 Dist. 1999). Also, a purpose of Rule 137, is to
prevent litigants from abusing the judicial process by penalizing the party
who initiates a vexatious or harassing action without a sufficient legal or
factual underpinning. In re Marriage of Pitulla, *256 Ill. App. 3d 84, 195 Ill.
Dec. 99, 628 N.E.2d 563, 1993 Ill. App. LEXIS 1768* (1 Dist. 1993). The
granting of sanctions under Supreme Court Rule 137 is entrusted to the
sound discretion of the trial court, and will   not be disturbed absent an
abuse of that discretion. *Fremarek v. John Hancock Mutual Life Insurance
Co.*, 272 Ill. App. 3d 1067, 1074, 651 N.E.2d 601, 209 Ill. Dec. 423 (1995).
A trial court exceeds its discretion only where no reasonable person would
take the view adopted by it. If reasonable people would differ as to the
propriety of the court's action, the reviewing court cannot say that the trial
court abused its discretion. *Fremarek*, 272 Ill. App. 3d at 1074.

In evaluating the conduct of an attorney, the court must determine
what was reasonable at the time rather than engage in hindsight. (*Lewy*,
211 Ill. App. 3d at 334-35.) Therefore, the standard to be employed in
applying the rule is an objective one. It is not sufficient that an attorney
"honestly believed" his or her case was well grounded in fact or law. *Shea,
Rogal & Associates, Ltd. v. Leslie Volkswagen, Inc.* (1993), 250 Ill. App. 3d
149, 153, 621 N.E.2d 77, 190 Ill. Dec. 208.

The conduct of the Plaintiffs and Snyder in this matter is
unexplainable. It is difficult to imagine the reasoning and logic that ran
through the mind of Ernest B. Fenton in requesting injunctive relief in this
matter in light of the fact that he knew that this matter had been removed
to federal court. Mr. Fenton touts himself as a Harvard Law School educated
lawyer and in his pleadings he states that his firm is highly sought after for
consumer related issues. Additionally, he states that his firm is sought after
for pro bono services, community speaking engagements, seminars and the

5

Subsequent to this series of events, others events took place concerning the instant matter. The defendants filed for a Supervisory Order with the Illinois Supreme Court requesting that this court be ordered to vacate the previously issued injunction and modification and the instant matter being remanded back to the Circuit Court of Cook County by the federal court.

Analysis

Illinois Supreme Court Rule 137 requires an attorney to certify that "he has read the pleading, motion, or other paper; that to the best of his knowledge, information, and belief formed after *reasonable inquiry* it is well grounded in fact and is warranted by existing law * * *" (134 Ill. 2d R.137.) (Emphasis added.) The purpose of the rule is to prevent abuse of the judicial process by penalizing claimants who bring vexatious and harassing actions based upon unsupported allegations of fact or law. It is not intended to simply penalize litigants for the lack of success; rather, its aim is to restrict litigants who plead frivolous or false matters without any basis in law. *Fischer v. Brombolich* (1993), 246 Ill. App. 3d 660, 664, 616 N.E.2d 743, 186 Ill. Dec. 553, *appeal denied,* 153 Ill. 2d 559, 624 N.E.2d 806; *Shea, Rogal & Associates, Ltd. v. Leslie Volkswagen, Inc.* (1993), 250 Ill. App. 3d 149, 153, 621 N.E.2d 77, 190 Ill. Dec. 208.

Pursuant to Ill. Sup. Ct. R. 137, a trial court may impose sanctions against a party or his counsel for filing a motion or pleading that is not well grounded in fact, not supported by existing law, or lacks a good-faith basis for modification, reversal, or extension of the law, or is interposed for any improper purpose as the purpose of Rule 137 is to prevent the filing of frivolous and false lawsuits. *Whitmer v. Munson,* 335 Ill. App. 3d 501, 269 Ill. Dec. 821, 781 N.E.2d 618, 2002 Ill. App. LEXIS 1122 (1 Dist. 2002). The purpose of Rule 137 is to penalize litigants who plead frivolous or false matters or bring suit without any basis in the law. *Morris B. Chapman &*

4

On July 17, 2013, the Plaintiffs, by one of their attorney's, Brian G. Snyder, appeared in the Circuit Court of Cook County, Sixth Municipal District and presented the Motion for Preliminary Injunction. That motion was signed by Ernest B. Fenton and not by Snyder. The defendants did not appear in court at this time concerning the motion. That matter was heard before the Honorable Loretta Eadie-Daniels at which time Snyder verbally advised her that the defendants had filed a Notice of Removal and tendered a copy of that Removal to Judge Daniels (Affidavit of Brian G. Snyder ¶ 7 as contained in Snyder's Submission in Opposition to the Entry of an Order Imposing Rule 137 Sanctions as Exhibit B.) Notwithstanding the fact that the motion should have been stopped dead in its tracks when it was first presented, it proceeded and after that presentment, it was granted and a 3 page order, prepared by Snyder, was entered.

The Order referenced the:

> "plaintiff's counsel being present; defendant not present; *the court being advised in the premises including the notice of removal filed by the defendants;*" (Emphasis added.)

Nearly a year later, on June 20, 2014, the Plaintiffs again appeared in court pursuant to a Motion Requesting Modification of a Preliminary Injunction. That modification was concerning the injunction that had been previously issued by Judge Eadie-Daniels on July 17, 2013. The matter was presented and the modification was granted by Judge Robert J. Clifford. Judge Clifford was not informed by the Plaintiffs that this matter had in fact been removed to federal court approximately one year prior and was still pending there at the time of the presentation of the Motion Requesting Modification of a Preliminary Injunction.

3

like in the community. It is hard to believe that a person with such a background would flout the law as he did and author and sign these pleadings and have a member of his firm present such a frivolous motion in court well knowing that the Circuit Court of Cook County had no jurisdiction to hear the matter.

Based upon a review of the record and pleadings and other submissions, it is inescapably concluded that Mr. Fenton's conduct in this matter is reprehensible. His conduct in relation to the presentment of the subject motion is quite disturbing as it has caused a considerable amount of consternation and unnecessary work (e.g. requesting Supervisory Orders) and time spent by the defendants, as well as this court, in addressing this matter. It is clear that Fenton did not have any belief, formed after *reasonable inquiry,* that it was well grounded in fact and was warranted by existing law. There was no jurisdiction and he knew it. He clearly abused the judicial process by having the motion, that he authored and signed, presented by a member of his firm (Snyder) in court well knowing that it was not proper. There is no way possible, nor absolutely no reason to believe, that Fenton "honestly believed" his motion was well grounded in fact or law as it had been removed to Federal Court. Additionally, Fenton has not provided this court with one iota of rationale or reasoning for his actions.

In light of the above, I find that no reasonable person would conclude that it was reasonable for Fenton to believe at the time he had the Motion presented in court by Snyder that the court would have had any jurisdiction to hear the matter much less grant an injunction.

Considering that a purpose of Rule 137 is to penalize litigants who plead frivolous or false matters or bring suit without any basis in the law, the presenting of a pleading, well knowing that the Court had no jurisdiction to hear it, screams for the imposition of a sanction.

6

As to Brian G. Snyder, he is really no less the culprit. Notwithstanding the fact that he did not author or sign the Motion, he presented it in court full well knowing that the case had been removed to Federal Court. He admits as much in his affidavit (¶7) and his email to Ms. Dudley in which he rather cavalierly states that he will advise the judge of the Notice of Removal and "We will leave it up to the judge to decide whether he wants to honor the Notice of Removal." What was he thinking? It is not up to the judge to decide whether or not to honor the removal of the case to federal court.

28 U.S.C. § 1446 deals with the procedure for removal of civil actions to federal court. In part it states:

> (d) Notice to adverse parties and State court. Promptly after the filing of such notice of removal of a civil action the defendant or defendants shall give written notice thereof to all adverse parties and shall file a copy of the notice with the clerk of such State court, *which shall effect removal* **and the State court shall proceed no further** *unless and until the case is remanded.* 28 U.S.C. § 1446(d) (Emphasis added).

Additionally, he was told by Dudley that sanctions would be sought if he proceeded with the motion in court.

Mr. Snyder in his Submission in Opposition to the Entry of an Order Imposing Rule 137 Sanctions tries to put forth a defense to the imposition of sanctions by relying on the fact that Rule 137 sanction are only to be imposed on the individual attorney who actually signed the pleading. *Au contraire.*

Snyder can take no solace from the fact his actions were oral rather than incorporated into a written pleading or motion. As the Appellate Court for the Fourth District noted, "The oral representations of an officer of the court, when in the form of a motion, should have the same effect as a signed, written motion within the context of section 2-611." *Modern Mailing*

7

Systems, Inc. v. McDaniels (1989) 191 Ill.App.3d 347, 351, 547 N.E.2d 762, 39 Ill.Dec 595. Numerous other courts in this state have recognized the close relationship between the written and the spoken word and applied Rule 137 or its predecessor to oral motions as well. (*Brubakken v. Morrison* (1992), 240 Ill. App. 3d 680, 684, 608 N.E.2d 471, 181 Ill. Dec. 398 ("Plainly, amended section 2-611 was intended to apply to all untrue statements given without reasonable cause to the court, whether active or passive, written or oral."); see also *State of Arizona ex rel. Painter v. Painter* (1992), 238 Ill. App. 3d 796, 803, 606 N.E.2d 298, 179 Ill. Dec. 466; *Lewy v. Koeckritz International, Inc.* (1991), 211 Ill. App. 3d 330, 334, 570 N.E.2d 361, 155 Ill. Dec. 848.)

To allow Snyder to stand in front of a judge and orally present the motion knowing that there was no jurisdiction for the court to entertain it, without consideration of the mandates of Rule 137 it would surely frustrate the very purpose of the rule and allow an attorney to make a mockery of our system of jurisprudence and send the wrong message to others that doing so would be tolerated.

During the course of all of this, Dudley and Sidea were put in a position of not being able to communicate with their own client due to the issuance of the injunction. They, by necessity, retained other attorneys to deal with the client, Ms. Davis. Mr. Robert Newman was retained to communicate with Ms. Davis so as not to violate the terms of the injunction. As a result of that, Mr. Newman became responsible for communication with Ms. Davis. As a result of this, certain legal fees were incurred by them. Additionally, Dudley expended time in dealing with this matter, including the injunction, the filing of motions, Supervisory Orders and the request for sanctions. Time spent and work performed on this wild goose chase initiated by the plaintiffs has caused strain on the court system and the defendants. The request for compensation is not unreasonable and is warranted based

8

upon the conduct of Fenton and Snyder.

In arriving at the sanction, this court has also taken into consideration the actions of Dudley and Sidea in their approach to handling this matter. Not appearing in court when the motion was presented has in part led to this abomination. Appearing may have nipped it in the bud. Also, there is no explanation as to why this matter was not brought to the attention of the federal judge presiding over the matter. If it was, this court was not made aware of that fact.

As a result of the egregious and recalcitrant behavior of Fenton and Snyder, sanctions are imposed as follows:

Earnest B. Fenton	$5,000.00
Brian G. Snyder	$1,000.00.

These amounts are to be paid directly to Ms. Dudley

DATED: June 6, 2016
ENTERED:

Associate Judge
Robert J. Clifford
JUN 0 6 2016
Circuit Court – 1902

Associate Judge
Robert J. Clifford No. 1902

9

The Judge who entered the gag order against me is no longer on the bench. She is not listed as an active attorney with the Illinois Attorney Discipline and Registration Commission (IARDC).

Besides advertising, scammers preyed on churches and on organizations that serve the African-American community. One attorney who did this eventually faced discipline from the IARDC, but kept going.

The Illinois Attorney General also filed suit, alleging there were 90 victims. Of these, 58 were African-American and 22 were Latinx. Only one was white.

Another frequent basis of targeting victims is ethnicity. Chicago is highly divided on ethnic grounds, so people who identify with a particular group are vulnerable. In a self-perpetuating cycle, they are shoved to the margins by the segregation and bigotry that prevails throughout the city and its surrounds. Then, they become increasingly reliant on people within the ethnic group —and vulnerable to anyone who speaks the same language or claims the same heritage or nationality.

One infamous scammer aggressively advertises he will "save your home." He works with an attorney who is not of the ethnic group, but has little enough self-respect to make his credentials available as a tool to defraud unsuspecting people. This scam goes a bit deeper than most: victims are actually persuaded to sign the deed to their property over to the scammer. The scammer falsely tells the victim that the banks and courts will be unable to figure out how to foreclose if the deed is no longer in the name of the homeowner being foreclosed upon. (Of course, it is really a simple matter for the bank to substitute the name of the new "owner" and continue the foreclosure.) Adding insult to injury, the scammer charges the victim for this "service." In variations of the scam, the scammer may charge rent for the person to live in his or her own home, evict the homeowner, sell the home to a third party, or simply let it go in the foreclosure—charging the homeowner legal fees for months or even years for an incompetent or non-existence "defense" to the foreclosure in court.

"Strategic" Default

Of course, some foreclosure defendants do not seem very sympathetic. Strategic default is a real phenomenon, though it was overly-trumpeted and misunderstood throughout the housing crisis. Strategic default, the idea that some homeowners intentionally missed payments to force their loan into default status or foreclosure, was bandied by many banks and judges as a reason to treat homeowners in a callous manner: they chose to miss payment and shouldn't be rewarded with humane treatment in court or realistic options to save the home. Using a broader stroke, those who brought on their financial problems (for example, by rolling pesky medical bills into their mortgage as part of a re-finance or by overspending on luxuries like food, medicine, and child care), also did not deserve due process. Affording them such would create a "moral hazard," leading everyone to default.

In fact, a significant cause of "strategic default" was the banks themselves. Customer service representatives often warned that the homeowner would not be considered for a modification or other relief while current. The homeowners would comply with the suggestion, only to find themselves standing in front of the freight train of foreclosure. The same banks would blanny that the slightest consideration for "due process" would lead to the "moral hazard" of a virtual homeowners' rent strike—masses of homeowners withholding payment for the joy of being tossed around a dirty, disorganized courthouse while begging for a day in court—or even a minute's consideration of a completed loan modification application.

Strategic defaults were also urged by "defense" attorneys. Those in distress—but not in foreclosure—would come to them, lured in by aggressive and misleading advertising. The attorneys would tell them to quit making mortgage payments, assuring a fore-closure would follow. The attorney would collect $1,500.00 (or more) each month while doing nothing to save the home from the foreclosure caused by the "legal advice." Meanwhile, the home-owner would know nothing of this until the Sheriff showed up to perform the eviction.

HEROES AND MONSTERS: NO WHITE HATS

" . . . that day Grandpa and I walked into the farm office/for a loan and this man didn't give my grandpa/an application because he was stupid, he said/because he was ignorant and inferior/and that moment/cut me in two torturous pieces/screaming my grandpa was a lovely man/that this government farm office clerk was a rude beast . . .". Jimmy Salvador Baca

Let Them Eat Graceful Exits

Whether intentions were good or bad, non-profit and governmental programs did not provide viable solutions to homeowners. Some were extremely well funded, with lawyers serving in roles that paid as well or better than private practice. In reality, governmental programs were used to dole out money to non-profit organizations. The money often carried a string, such as placing limits on what advice could be given. Unfortunately, some lawyers had enough disrespect for their license and oath as attorneys to give incomplete information without disclosing this to the homeowner to allow an opportunity to seek further, nonbiased advice.

One example of a misleading program is the extremely well-funded Cook County Mortgage Foreclosure Mediation Program. Even where some organizations meant well, the judiciary, with an obscure "committee," directed and limited the kind of advice given, often with devastating results. For example, judges would direct homeowners to paid staff sitting in the hallways of the Daley Center courthouse. While holding themselves out with the indicia of judicial approval, the paid staff were not allowed to tell people they had not been properly served. There is nothing wrong with any attorney not offering a service or type of advice —simply saying, "There may be an issue here, but I cannot advise you." However, here, people were required to file answers to take part in the highly-touted, well-funded "mediation" program —and doing so waived their objections to jurisdiction without them ever having been alerted they had rights. They were stuffed through the system, into a lucrative (for the "non profits") sausage casing.

One legal aid organization that was part of the program offered to help a homeowner in court as long as he gave up his defenses and agreed to move. This "graceful exit" strategy predominated the program. However, it begs the question: for whom was it graceful? The homeowner ended up homeless, the goal of the plaintiff filing the foreclosure. That leaves the plaintiff, who was spared the trouble of doing the legal work to prove its case.

This same organization said that, in some cases, it would offer post-mediation litigation services through the Access to Justice program if the foreclosure did not settle at mediation. However, in the flow of the program, one was required to file an answer (and those filed invariably admitted away all substantive defenses) before participating. Whatever litigation could be done would be largely ineffective to save the home.

To the Guillotine

By any guess, an invitation to speak at Harvard would be a peak in a legal career. Around 2010, with the help of friends from the Chicago Anti-Eviction Campaign, I was invited to speak at a conference hosted by Harvard's legal aid clinic.

The topic of my talk was to be foreclosure mediation. Since I had strong criticism of the Cook County foreclosure mediation program, I invited a student of mine who was an intern (and, later, enthusiastic staff member of) at one of the leading programs in the mediation and Access to Justice programs. He was able to provide a counterpoint to my criticisms in what became a panel presentation. I presented accurate information, such as that the success rate publicized by the mediation program was largely composed of "graceful exit" agreements. I posited that the program could help far more people per dollar by dividing monies spent on the program among homeowners for direct assistance. Money could be used to reinstate the mortgage, to pay part of the arrears as part of a modification, or to hire competent legal representation. Any of these would have saved more homes that the mediation and Access to Justice programs, saving the over $111,000.00 spent on the mediation program director alone.

As I became vocal about concerns some of the programs were not serving homeowners well, I also cited incorrect and incomplete information distributed by the Advice Desk. Some of the answers they helped homeowners prepare did not effectively preserve the homeowners' defenses. In some cases, homeowners were told they "had to" file the answer without being informed of the possibility of seeking other counsel to explore rights arising from improper service of process or incorrect allegations in the foreclosure complaint.

Around that time, a friend of mine was recruited on to a "court advisory committee" that was part of (what was later found to be) a system in which the court would dictate what information homeowners were to be told. The committee consisted of plaintiffs' attorneys and a couple of particularly milquetoast "defense" attorneys. While the plaintiffs' attorneys all worked for profit, the defense side was limited almost exclusively to those working for non-profit organizations easily controlled by the funding stream distributed by the foreclosure mediation program. My friend asked why I was not part of the committee and was told by the director of the foreclosure mediation program that I was "crazy."

In the same vein, I was invited by the law school where I then taught to make a presentation to a group of students and professors volunteering for Access to Justice, another well-funded program cooperating with the mediation program. As I began my talk, the director, an employee of the Chicago Bar Foundation, shut me down. In front of the students and my colleagues she stated, "We will not be discussing ANY of your 'defense' stuff here!" I was not allowed to speak throughout the presentation, and my school was told that allowing me to talk to the students--attendees of the school that employed me as a program coordinator and adjunct professor--they would be cut from the Access to Justice program. Even comparatively mundane concerns I raised, like cautioning against a rising trend of young attorneys using mediation conferences to flirt with the attorney from the other side, prioritizing interest in a future date over client needs, were shut down.

As I became more vocal about my concerns with the programs, the reports that I was "crazy" spread. I was excluded from programs, including those I founded or led. An online forum where I contributed many helpful articles and forms took down my content and replaced it with misleading information from an

attorney who worked for a well-heeled non-profit legal aid organization where he regularly told people in trouble, especially
those facing condominium foreclosures and evictions, they had
no legal recourse (an untrue assertion).

Of course, as the truth came out, the program was interested in
funneling money. The program was a
sausage casing into which homeowners were stuffed - creating a
lucrative sausage for chosen non-profit organizations. Staff and
funding recipients were often selected according to Cook County
patronage practices, with the result that a dismal number of
homes were saved in view of the money spent. It was mercifully
euthanized when the Cook County Commissioners cut funding
for the Cook County courts.

LC: A bankruptcy trustee betrays trust

The bankruptcy trustee's position is one of . . . well, trust. This
powerful, court-appointed attorney represents the creditors'
interest in bankruptcy. In a Chapter 7 bankruptcy, the alleged
debtor gives up possessions (except for a few that fall within
statutory exceptions) in exchange for discharge of debts. The
trustee is supposed to collect and account for the possessions
and divide them equitably (usually following a sale) among the
creditors. Unless it qualifies for an exception, the alleged debtor's
home is included in this "bankruptcy estate." In other words, the
home is normally sold and the proceeds divided among creditors.
Many lawyers routinely fail to explain the difference between a
Chapter 7 and a Chapter 13 bankruptcy to clients. Some lawyers'
neglect of the distinction between these two bankruptcy tools
makes any educated (make that: any conscious) person wonder
if they know the difference themselves. Since a Chapter 13 generally provides for allowing one to keep one's "house, car, and
possessions" (a phrase routinely trumpeted in a style reminiscent

of hawkers of worthless "snake-oil" remedies), the difference between Chapter 13 and Chapter 7 is important. A person seeking
to keep his worldly goods intact will be sorely disappointed if a
Chapter 7 is filed, causing relinquishment of "house, car, and possessions."

This is exactly what happened to LC, a young African-American
woman from the south side of Chicago. A real go-getter, LC helped
a colleague repair homes and had purchased and repaired her own
home. She had a beautiful place to live until she fell behind on
a few payments and hired an attorney seeking to line his own
pockets as part of his trajectory to the top. He eventually became
a judge.

LC was one of my first clients, and I was eager to help her.
Major servicing issues in her case made it clear the bank had not
credited her payments. The foreclosure was entirely illusory—LC
had not really defaulted. Compared to some of the complex fact
patterns I faced, saving LC's home would be easy. About all that
was required was to show the receipts for her timely payments. If
showing them to the opposing counsel did not help, then I would
take them to the court. LC could quite possibly save her home
and win money from the other side or its lawyers.

However, one factor made LC's home impossible to save. She had
gone to another attorney before me. Investigating the facts, the
attorney (now judge) had filed for a Chapter 7 bankruptcy for
LC. LC had unknowingly relinquished title to her home to the
bankruptcy trustee! In the pre-electronic-documents era, it took
a long time to find out the status of LC's case. Mr. Attorney Judge
responded to my inquiries with a letter stating his-future-honor
did not "need" my aspersions. I tersely responded LC did not
"need" to have her home stolen!

Despite the obstacles, I put up a vigorous defense and was able to
get the attention of a seasoned attorney at the bank's law firm.

He provided me with the file—wherein the fact of the Chapter 7 bankruptcy was clear. To be clear, this was not in any way the fault of the foreclosing bank or its attorneys. Mr. Attorney Judge had simply taken LC's money (several thousand dollars) on a promise of saving her home, and proceeded to file the very paperwork that forfeited the home. He never attended a single court date in state court or in bankruptcy court.

Desperate to help LC, I contacted the bankruptcy trustee responsible for collecting her assets. After several rounds of negotiation, the trustee agreed to re-convey LC's house to her—in exchange for payment. Miraculously, LC was able to arrange the payment. However, LC never regained her home. Well before the contract's expiration—and after I notified the trustee that LC would be able to purchase her home—the trustee sold the home to one of his cronies.

There were no repercussions whatsoever for the trustee or for the attorney who handled the matter for LC. To the contrary, the trustee is now an attorney in private practice. He "defends" foreclosures. Do call him if you ever need to "save your home." And, of course, Mr. Attorney Judge shot to his place on the bench.

DL: When we want your name, we'll give it to you

DL had one of the most compelling cases I have ever encountered. This homeowner was forced into foreclosure on false pretenses because the lender simply did not like or understand the homeowner's last name and unilaterally changed it at the closing table. DL, an immigrant, bore two last names associated with cultural tradition. The bank chose the first of the two last names and placed it on loan documents. At the closing table, DL objected to their documents bearing the wrong name., but was told to sign the documents "as is" if he wanted the loan. Since he had a contract to buy a home that would be in breach that day if he did not take the loan, he followed instructions. Later, DL made homeowners insurance payments to a local insurance broker who knew him by his correct name. Since the bank required DL to maintain insurance under the terms of the loan, it asked for verification DL had the insurance. When DL (and, eventually, the insurance broker) repeatedly sent the proof of insurance, it was under the real name, not the name arbitrarily assigned to DL by the mortgage company. The mortgage company refused to recognize the proof of insurance and eventually "force placed" insurance on the home, causing the monthly payment to skyrocket. Force-placed insurance is insurance bought by a lender, usually from a crony company. It only insures the lender's interest in the home - not the homeowners' equity or belongings - but costs much more than typical homeowners' insurance. The cost is passed along to the homeowner, who is declared in default if it is not paid as part of the monthly mortgage payment.

DL was finally held in default. Following the directions on his summons, he went to Daley Center Courthouse to access services for people in foreclosure. When DL approached the Advice Desk, no one was available to provide service in Spanish. Rather than arranging for a return visit when a Spanish speaker was available, the then-director of the desk provided a blank "foreclosure answer" and told DL he "had to" file it, marking an X in each spot where he should sign. Understanding a little bit of this English, DL filed the answer, waiving all of the arguments that could have been made on in the case.

Finally, DL got a private foreclosure "defense" lawyer. Paying nearly $1,000.00 per month, he was not informed of any action the lawyer took. The lawyer did not file any paperwork and even threatened DL with arrest when he visited the lawyer's office to ask about the status of the case. After that incident, the lawyer wrote letters, *ex parte* communications that were not copied to DL as legally required, to the judge and opposing counsel warning that extra security was needed in court each time DL appeared. This cast a bad light on the client and utterly violated every duty a lawyer might have to a client. Perhaps most damaging, he abjectly refused to return the file to the client, even when ordered to do so by the Court.

When I appeared, I moved to withdraw the bad answer provided by the Advice Desk. The opposing counsel wrote a 77-page brief about my laziness and inability to follow timelines (about 30 days into my representation). By some miracle, the judge granted the motion to withdraw the bad answer. The judge commented she supposed the Advice Desk was "better than nothing," to which I replied it was much, much worse than nothing. After a lengthy struggle, I was able to file a good answer, and we also settled a separate civil rights case.

As a sad postscript, however, simply withdrawing a bad answer is not always enough. The bad answer is still considered a "judicial admission" and often results in summary judgment in favor of the bank. There is almost nothing that can be done to undo the incompetence visited upon homeowners when a lawyer or legal aid organization provides a bad answer to a mortgage foreclosure complaint.

SF: Left her mother's death bed to face an arrest threat

SF was a determined fighter faced with a decision about her home following a divorce and income reduction. On her first court date, her mother was spending her final few days in a hospital bed. SF would have liked to have been by her mother's side, but she and her minor daughter obeyed the paperwork (a notice of motion for summary judgment) they had received. When they stepped up in court and asked for more time in their home, they were directed to the Advice Desk. Mother and daughter proceeded to the Desk and were directed to a seating area. Concerned about her daughter, the mother asked if she could take her daughter for lunch and return without losing her place and was told she could. They returned and waited for hours, seeing many who had come later going in for service. Finally, SF asked if her number would be soon. She was told no one else would be seen that day. When she began crying, her papers were wrenched from her and she was physically thrust to the door, her terrified daughter following.

Determined to follow the judge's direction to visit the Advice Desk, SF returned. This time, she was escorted in to see the very same paid staff member who had ordered her removal. She was not allowed to sit and was made to stand at the door of the paid staff member's cubicle (because she was, allegedly, a physical threat to the paid staff member). The paid attorney rustled through papers and declared the pending matter was a motion for summary judgment and said, "Defendants don't have to file a response." In fact, defendants must file good, thorough responses or lose their homes at this point. As SF did with advice rendered on your tax dollar.

VIOLATIONS OF TRUST

"*I f one really wishes to know how justice is admin-
istered in a country, one does not question the po-
licemen, the lawyers, the judges, or the protected
members of the middle class. One goes to the unprotected-
those, precisely, who need the laws's protection most!-and
listens to their testimony.*" James Baldwin

The Private Bar (Defense)

A post-note to LC's case above is that I arrived in court one day
to present a motion asking the judge to grant us an order forbid-
ding the scammers who stole her deed from selling property. Opposing counsel did not show up. We waited. I called. (Typically,
judges and sheriffs officers make snide comments and threaten to
take cell phones brought into the courtroom. If a homeowner is
late to court, the case is heard, the home is taken, and requests
to recall the case are denied even if the opposing counsel is still
in the courtroom. However, when bank lawyers are late, homeowners and their attorneys are usually forced to wait for hours
and sometimes required to use their personal cell phones--the
same ones that can be the subject of so much vitriol--to track
down opposing counsel.) We waited. Finally, the judge set the
case over to be heard in a couple of days to see if I could awaken

the apparently snoozing legal genius. Several days hence, at the re-set hearing, my many calls and faxes had received no answer. Opposing counsel was still a no-show. My motion was granted.

A few weeks later, we found out what happened: the lawyer had been arrested. He took part in a scam exactly like the one at issue in LC's case, but with several other scammers—a family dubbed "The Jackson Five" had decided they would find their fortunes in theft of property rather than in music, and their lawyer played bass as a full-fledged band member! He got to do a stint providing prison entertainment and lost his license to practice law.

The Plaintiffs' Bar

Plaintiffs' attorneys represented banks, lenders, investors, and servicers seeking to take homes through the foreclosure process. Generally, one plaintiff's attorney was as good as the next and there was no real need to wish them ill. After all, if one disappeared, another would pop up. Most of them failed to distinguish themselves and were utterly fungible. A few good guys (in this largely male field) did more to save homes that all the "non-profit" initiatives put together. This did not usually involve heroics, simply listening to hear that the address was wrong, the complaint was missing information, the plaintiff had failed to account for payments that were actually made on time, or other factual issues. In any other area of law, listening to the facts from the other side and working to resolve issues is unremarkable. However, foreclosure plaintiff's lawyers often came to court with 50 or 60 files to be heard on one call (in front of one judge in one hour or two period). This left little time for worrying about details like whether a homeowner was actually in default. In addition, many large firms refused to delegate enough problem solving discretion to the attorneys. This often trapped good attorneys on a hamster wheel of professional responsibility violations that many abandoned, leading to a constant deluge of new, untrained attorneys handling sensitive matters.

The biggest disincentive for plaintiff attorney competence, however, was the industry's success in lobbying for change. Through the court's "foreclosure committee" and through the legislature, virtually any gain made by homeowners was wiped out by legislative change or judicial fiat. For example, at one point, "standing" was a good argument. It questioned whether a bank that had acquired a mortgage and note from the original lender had properly documented its right to foreclose—showing it actually held the mortgage. This is no different than any other case—standing is required for the court to have jurisdiction over a matter. It is laughably simple to most people that I cannot sue a motorist who hits a third party in a car accident unless I am injured myself. (I may be able to sue for lack of consortium or emotional distress, but those are injuries to me. I cannot sue for someone else's broken leg.) However, at the height of the crisis, banks were foreclosing willy nilly, with no regard for whether they actually held the right to foreclose. The road to change was somewhat complex because one source of frustration arose from the "defense" bar— just as the banks willy nilly filed foreclosures, some attorneys filed a motion to dismiss based on the standing argument without making any effort to be sure it applied in the particular case at hand or even to edit the document to reflect the particulars of an individual case. A quick Google search for "standing foreclosure defense" brings up a cuckoo's nest of foreclosure "defense" lawyers and demonstrates the overuse of this theory to bring in and extract money from vulnerable clients. In the end, the courts put an end to the theory (at least in Illinois' first appellate district) in 2010 with *Mers v. Barnes*. This was to the detriment of homeowners who had had the title to their home scrambled by alleged assignments of their mortgage and transfer of their note. At present, judges have actually held that the rules of civil procedure do not apply to the mortgage foreclosure cases notwithstanding the fact that the Illinois Mortgage Foreclosure Law is embodied entirely in the Illinois Rules of Civil Procedure. And, they have ruled people can only protest personal jurisdiction within 60 days, despite the age-old rule that it is up to the plaintiff to acquire and prove personal jurisdiction. It is mind-boggling to anyone who had practiced in any other area of law that the court would exercise personal jurisdiction to declare it has personal jurisdiction over someone when it has no jurisdiction to find anything! Other decisions and statutes have demanded defendants—even *pro se* ones—use greater particularity in answering the complaint to avoid judicial admissions and requiring, in some court rooms, defendants to "prove" (using an affidavit) the "need" the discovery guaranteed to all litigants in Illinois.

Most of the abuses set forth above are abuses of power—using access and cronyism to tilt outcomes in favor of one's own side. While abhorrent, it is the Chicago way. Not following it could probably get one exiled from the kingdom built on hot dogs and poor taste. Some abuses were related to specific litigation.

Early on, I had a student volunteer (extern) accompany me to court. I met a lawyer in court and extended my hand. He refused my hand and sneered, "What do you want?" All I had done was file my appearance, so, while capable of earning a good sneer, I had not done so in this case. I replied that I thought I would represent my client. The student was taken aback and ended up writing her paper on civility.

Perhaps one of the funniest incidents was fighting with a lawyer who was too bigoted to go to the property (located on the south side of Chicago) upon which his client sought to foreclose. The property was a large commercial tract, and the lawyer's firm represented the bank at the time the mortgage was extended as well as in the foreclosure. They made the mistake of only attaching the mortgage to a few interior parcels of this multi-parcel property. I wanted to figure out if the bank vice president the lawyer had disclosed as his primary witness knew his lien was only attached to the "hole" and was surrounded by a donut of property my client owned free and clear. I often joked we should allow the foreclosure and charge the bank a toll to cross over my client's donut to access their holding. Curious as to what his response would be if I asked him to walk the area he thought was at issue in the case, I noticed his deposition for the property location. The lawyer wrote to me, "As you know, depositions in Illinois must proceed in downtown Chicago." I replied, "Wow! That must be a problem for people in Carbondale!"

Ultimately, the lawyer did not produce Mr. Vice President. When my motion to compel was up, the judge was clearly frustrated. Sensing the racism at play, the judge announced they would be required to go to my office—one in an area racists would consider a "worse" neighborhood than that of my client. On the appointed day, Mr. Lawyer and Mr. Vice President rolled up looking like idiots in some kind of oversized SUV and parked conspicuously near the building, clearly fearing for their lives in walking to my door! I completed the deposition, and (using a survey) it was clear Mr. Vice President had no idea of his downtown law firm buddy's mistakes.

We lost at trial, the judge granting the foreclosure on the parcels that actually were secured by the mortgage. It still seemed clear Mr. Lawyer had kept his client in the dark. Finally, I turned the file back to my client's usual corporate attorney. Throughout the litigation, we had offered to pay $150,000.00 to settle the case. After the case concluded, the bank apparently found out how they had been deceived. They ultimately accepted $50,000.00 to release what little interest they had in the property. It was an expensive win for them.

In an almost equally silly case, I assisted a client who was in the Cook County Mortgage Foreclosure Mediation Program. Part of the process was tendering particular financial documents to the Plaintiff's foreclosure firm. My client meticulously gathered the reams of paper required. When I informed the opposing counsel, a lawyer at a large plaintiff's foreclosure firm, the papers were ready, she was unable to accept them by facsimile transmittal and claimed to be unable to open email attachments. I suggested I send them by next-day mail or Federal Express. She had the gall to claim the firm could not receive mail. Knowing she was lying, and unwilling to sacrifice my client's home on the altar of her deception, I mailed the documents to the firm, marking them to the attention of a trustworthy litigator there. I sent him an email message asking him to kindly drop off the documents at my opposing counsel's desk. The tactic worked: my client got his loan modification and continues to live in his home ten years later, and a new bar was set for mail room or messenger salaries at the law firm.

Systemic Problems

Of all the factors contributing to the loss of homes that were easily savable, the Cook County Mortgage Foreclosure Mediation Program was the worst offender. This highly-touted program was established to help homeowners, but the director quickly told the press it was not a "save your home" program. New participants, homeowners who received a foreclosure summons which directed them to contact the program, were herded into a "training" session. The very first substantive slide and page in their workbook asked, "Why am I in foreclosure?" The answer appeared on the next slide, "Because you failed to make a mortgage payment." The word "alleged" was missing, no discussion of defenses was had, and other possible allegations leading to foreclosure (such as alleged failure to maintain homeowners' insurance) were discussed.

Confused litigants asking for help in court were directed to program managers seated directly outside the courtroom in the corridors of the courthouse. The managers had been indoctrinated that there were no defenses to foreclosure. I was invited to one of the early training sessions for program volunteers, held at a law school where I was adjunct faculty, and, at that time, staff—directing the predatory lending program that provided free brief legal advice to people in foreclosure and dispatched students to assist HUD-certified housing counseling agencies. When I began to explain the defenses to foreclosure and how to answer a complaint, a Chicago Bar Foundation representative shut me down. Inexplicably pooching out her lips as she talked, she stated there would be "none of your defense stuff" in the session. My law school was later told that if I was allowed to talk to students about foreclosure defense, their participation in the Access to Justice program would be ended. Because this was a critical component of a *pro bono* program the school was attempting to start, it capitulated to the demand students' access to me be curtailed. This ensured not only the mediation program would not fulfill its stated mission, but that students hoping to be competent foreclosure defense lawyers were denied a significant resource.

At the training, instead of my "defense stuff," the directors—affiliated with a highly-funded nonprofit, the mediation program, the Chicago Bar Foundation, and the "Access to Justice" Program (another highly funded device to misinform homeowners and ensure loss of their homes)—imparted to students that there was no defense to foreclosure and they would be helping people negotiate a "graceful exit." A graceful exit, was, apparently, graceful for the banks—who did not have to go through the messy eviction process. Homeowners were persuaded to leave their homes, turn over their keys, and not fight for the home. Of course, persuading them that they were guilty—not allegedly guilty—of a payment default, failing to analyze other allegations of default (like false allegations of failure to maintain homeowners insurance), and failing to discuss defenses made it difficult for the homeowners to ever assert their rights. In fact, a condition of participating in the mediation program was to file an answer before asking to be referred to the program. The answers were filed *pro se* and without any competent legal consultation in most cases. The people staffing the tables to provide "help" in the courtroom hallways were almost all lawyers admitted to practice in Illinois. However, they were forbidden from so much as telling people that service upon them was insufficient. Homeowners were often tricked into giving away jurisdictional objections, defenses, and counterclaims as a prerequisite for participation in the mediation program. The program wrote the answers, the answers gave away the defenses, the lack of a defense ensured a "graceful exit" at best, and, most importantly, staff got paid and grostesquely funded organizations became moreso.

The inadequacy of the program's approach was made clear when I accompanied one of few clients I had who took part in the mediation program to his mediation session. I saw a colleague from the law school where I was shut down at the program training with her client. We exchanged pleasantries and accompanied our respective clients into separate mediation rooms at about the same time. I had filed a thorough answer for my client, posited counterclaims, and engaged in exhaustive discovery. As a result, the bank's attorney from the foreclosure firm appeared, but an attorney from a respected outside "litigation" firm also attended. When we left our session, there were hugs all around. My client was elated. He was offered a modification that had even better terms than his original mortgage and was in the rare position of being better off after the foreclosure process than before it. Sadly, my colleague and her client appeared at the same time. There were no hugs as the tearful homeowner made her way to the elevator.

SEEKING JUSTICE

*"**A**gainst eternal injustice, man must assert justice, and to protest against the universe of grief, he must create happiness." Albert Camus*

Some of us diligently sought justice even if our paths diverged from time to time. I was lucky to work with several community groups. At one time, I spoke, at no cost, to homeowners in foreclosure four nights per week and at least one day on the weekend. I would give a presentation and then sit with attendees, answering individual legal questions, providing incredibly detailed sample pleadings, and reviewing foreclosure paperwork until the sponsoring organization or building kicked us out. Because tactics could differ, I sometimes excused myself as activist tactics were discussed, distinguishing myself from at least one self-righteous snob from an extremely well-funded "legal aid" organization who would take up the group's time centering herself and preaching about her inability to endorse this or that tactic. Sometimes I was with the Chicago Anti-Eviction Campaign at 11:00 pm or even 2:00 am.

CAEC was one of the organizations really working to improve life for those most affected by foreclosure. Though it, I met, among others, Willie (JR) Fleming and Toussaint Losier. They were both committed housing activists, not just passing through to build a power base to export to another "movement" when the tides of the press and funding shifted. When I sued "defense" attorneys and scammers in foreclosure, witnesses who came to me with tales of woe jumped ship like the rats they were when subpoenas came out. Bearing excuses from just being a stupid, scared 30-some year old child (with a law degree and a penchant for gloating about money and power) to claiming threats from the opposition, even lawyers refused to show up to tell judges about the ruination caused by those who preyed on people in foreclosure. Not JR Fleming! He showed up, testified, and said his piece in the trial of a notorious scammer, being one factor in our win. He did not stretch out his hand for money, claim fear of reprisal, or simply assert he was too important to give a little time to improve the legal system. In this way, he remained head and shoulders above lawyers who crow about their money and power while clinging to a job they say disenfranchises them from testifying.

One night, I missed a CAEC meeting. Driving past the meeting place later, I felt an urge to call Toussaint, a leader in the group. Toussaint was relieved to hear from me and asked me to come to the meeting place—they were still there at 11:00 pm. A home-owner, Ms. B, had come to the meeting with a problem. She had resolved her foreclosure by reinstating her property—paying off the amount the bank said she owed as past due payment, late fees, attorney fees, court costs, and whatever other malarkey they could dream up. She had a receipt, a letter confirming the loan was reinstated, a new payment book, and business cards of those who had taken the payment.

Even though Ms. B had been assured the foreclosure would be dismissed and her future payments accepted, she saw her property listed in the back of a local paper in the "legal notices" section as about to be subject to judicial sale. One of the "legal fictions" (lies) necessary to the foreclosure system is that tiny ads in the back of newspapers provide notice to those subject to proceedings. Ms. B truly beat the system by seeing the ad and acting on it even though she had just two days to save her home. I prepared sample motions to stay the sale and provided Ms. B with information about navigating the courthouse and the complicated procedures for setting up an emergency motion. Toussaint was on standby to help her navigate and avoid the various "programs" inside the courthouse that would all but take the home for the bank, probably telling her to go home and pack!

As I worked, I discreetly sent email messages about the situation to everyone I knew at the foreclosing law firm. I did not want to get Ms. B's hopes up, and, more importantly, any inkling on her part that she should wait for an email response would jettison her opportunity to get an emergency hearing.

We worked with Ms. B until about 2:00 am. The next morning, I had a court date for someone else in DuPage County. As I left court, about 9:30 am, I had a series of email messages and a phone call from a senior lawyer in the foreclosing law firm. There were apologies and a promise to cancel the sale and dismiss the case. I was able to reach Ms. B and Toussaint just before they made it all the way downtown.

This is what real community organizing does. Of course, my employer simply questioned whether I had done enough hours. One secretary, who used tearing me down as her entire career strategy, decided we didn't provide the entire service within a targeted economic zone (empowerment zone). We actually were well within the zone. At another point, the same secretary determined I would never meet our grant's requirement of doing X presentations because I was "not doing enough." Simple math showed we were 1/4 of the way through the grant year yet I had done over 1/2 of the required work for the year. She declined my offers to allow her take over my job of driving all over Chicago all night and all weekend, responding to panicked homeowner calls at all hours.

To this day, I don't think Ms. B cares whether I worked 40 hours or 50 hours per week when I was only paid for 30 or if her home was in the "empowerment zone." I picture her in her house, happy.

CAEC was not the only organization doing good work. After years of informally helping people in foreclosure by giving talks and brief individual advice in conjunction with community organizations, I started a small clinic, Resistance Legal Clinic. In particular, I was urged on by Thomas Hansen of Centro Autonomo in the Albany Park neighborhood of Chicago. Plans were hatched at his dinner table and Centro provided space and support for initial meetings.

A small cohort of students came forward to help those in foreclosure or with similar housing concerns. One of our focal points was keeping people away from the various "helping" projects discussed above. Many of these took up tax-payer funded space in the Daley Center courthouse but were almost certain to steer homeowners wrong, hastening home loss.

Around the time we started Resistance, I provided a woman referred by a sincere HUD-certified housing counseling agency with a set of sample pleadings to allow her to fight her foreclosure. She had not received proper service of process, faced several Federal Debt Collection Practices Act violations by the foreclosing law firm, and needed guidance to assert her rights and save her home. In addition to sample pleadings, I provided her with instructions on how to file and present needed paperwork. I charged her nothing. My help would allow her to effectively defend the foreclosure case while she worked with the housing counselor to modify her loan or get her payments on track.

While at the courthouse, the homeowner, Mrs. F, became confused about the location of the Clerk of Court's office. She needed to go there to file documents. Unfortunately, she stumbled across the paid employees, who were also attorneys admitted to practice law, associated with the mediation program. They examined my pleadings, told Mrs. F they were "a scam" and provided her with a form answer and appearance that would give up all her defenses to the foreclosure she lost her home.

When Mrs. F found the Clerk's office, she coincidentally encountered the best possible clerk. Mrs. F handed the Clerk all the papers--the ones she had prepared from my samples and those the well-paid mediation attorneys had foisted upon her. The Clerk flipped through the stack of documents, stamped the ones prepared with my assistance, folded the ones the vultures urged on the litigant, and handed the documents back to her. The Clerk, legally prohibited from giving legal advice, urged Mrs. F to contact me.

Mrs. F called me in tears from the courthouse hallway. Terrified she had filed the vulture's dung, I met with her the next day. Mrs. F had been saved by Clerk's actions--the competent pleadings prepared with my help were filed. Those pushed on her by the highly-paid program attorneys were not. Had she filed the latter, she would have submitted to the Court's jurisdiction despite not having been served, admitted away all of her defenses, and almost certainly lost her home in short order.

Going forward, Resistance volunteers accompanied people to the courthouse. Students could not provide legal advice or service, but they performed a critical function: ensuring homeowners did not become ensnared by those who accepted pay and sereptitiously undermined the homeowners who depended on them. Probably making it most clear that the powers that be did not like our work--actually saving homes rather than passing out platitudes and hastening homelessness--was an incident in which we were offered money to shut up. Unfortunately, none of us working sincerely to save homes understood the unspoken language that we were to silence our criticisms.

Several groups had urged the Illinois Attorney General to support real community efforts, prosecute fraudsters in the mortgage and foreclosure rescue arenas, and support laws to protect home-

owners. Particularly troublesome, the Attorney General fre-
quently entered into settlements with wrongdoers that accrued
far too little to the benefit of homeowner victims. For example,
money was often doled out to crony organizations rather than
going directly to the homeowners hurt by particular scams.

Attorney General staff showed up at one of our meetings. I was
being honored by a group for my consistent help, at no charge,
with saving homes alongside the organization. The AG staff en-
thusiastically urged us to participate in an upcoming grant cycle.

Three organizations joined forces, and I worked with another
lawyer who supported Resistance to write the grant application.
Of course, working with community groups and volunteers was
like herding cats and requests for resumes, timelines, and corporate paperwork required multiple trips, email messages, and
phone calls. However, we pulled an application together. Working on the application took time, interfering with my ability to
help with individual cases for several weeks (and leading to a
clash with one organization who expected me to "drop everything" on the day the application was due to help a homeowner
they had identified). Similarly, the affected organizations were
busy, having to call off a protest and several actions. We did not
realize it at the time, but we were kept occupied and gave the AG
a respite.

We turned in a complete application. Months passed, then we
were summarily turned down. The application had supposedly
been evaluated by the Illinois Housing Development Authority--
a funding source for many of the anti-homeowner efforts discussed above.

Although we did not win, our ideas--accompanying homeowners
to the courthouse as escorts, helping in the community rather
than at brick-and-mortar sites, and others--were soon picked up
by the organizations that did win the money. We learned a hard

lesson about doing capitalism's busy work.

DORMANT PLAGUE

> **"** *... the plague bacillus never dies or disappears for good ... it can lie dormant for years and years in furniture and linen chests ... it bides its time in bedrooms, cellars, trunks, and bookshelves; and that perhaps the day [will] come when, for the bane and the enlightening of men, it [will] rouse up its rats again and send them forth to die in a happy city."* Albert Camus

There are plenty of articles on the coming foreclosure crisis, a housing crisis likely to exceed the 2006 meltdown. I am not examining the data in support of this here.

However, rest assured the crisis is coming.

The courts remain as unprepared as ever to deal with an influx of foreclosure cases. While online filing has been mandated in Cook County, the Clerk of Court is unable to handle filing in any kind of reasonable way. In May 2019, I made multiple attempts to file an additional appearance for a client whose fee had been waived due to financial need. Normally, an additional appearance does not require a fee. Even if there was one, this client had a waiver. For two reasons, the filing should have been free. However, the clerk repeatedly rejected the filing until I walked it in to the office in person.

At the same time, I filed a motion to vacate the judgment against the same client. Again, despite the fee waiver, I was charged $60.00 after a long struggle to have the clerk stamp the time-sensitive document at all. Finally, a clerk determined one of my filings could not be accepted without "leave of court." Neither my client nor I were afforded any due process, and this is a determination that should be made by a judge, not a clerk. In fact, the motion I was not allowed to file was proper. My opposing counsel saw a copy and, knowing my client would likely prevail, made a settlement offer that allowed us to avoid having to petition the court to tell the clerk's office to do its job.

As a final inconvenience, opposing counsel and I arrived in court only to find the clerk's automated system (which has no override option) had set the court date my motion to vacate and ten or more motions by other attorneys in the wrong courtroom. This made work for the judge to redirect us, and, absent our agreement informally resolving the case, would have required additional days wrangling with the clerk and appearing in the correct courtroom for my opposing counsel, our clients, and me.

Given the above, I cannot fathom how an unrepresented person will navigate a complex case. This is complicated by the fact almost none of the shortcomings I point out in the book have been resolved. To the contrary, many "dedicated" non-profits reduced or closed down housing efforts as press attention and grant funds dwindled. One particularly sycophantic group abruptly cancelled free foreclosure education seminars with no notice to me, the venue, or potential clients. I had been providing free educational sessions for the group several times per week (and all weekend), and showed up at a public library to find no program staff from the organization. I provided information to the ten or so people in foreclosure who had hoped to attend. Following up with the group, I found they had met the number of presentations required by the grant and simply quit running the program without notice--on to the next revenue stream! Other organizations simply followed the press vans and money stream to prison justice work, to which they will, no doubt, be dedicated until the tide shifts. (A few organizations like Uptown Peoples Law Center and individuals like Chicago activist Holly Krig have ably worked in both areas for many years, and I do not include them in this criticism.)

Other organizations simply fired staff, often focusing on those most integral to housing. Notably, the Cook County Foreclosure Mediation Program fell to budget cuts, and one can only hope it will not be resurrected in light of the swath of empty homes left in its wake throughout its existence.

CONCLUSION

The chancery court is the division of the court where foreclosures are heard. Historically, this is a court empowered to "do equity" between parties where more than mere money is at stake.

In the case of the foreclosure crisis, systems worked together to deprive people of equity. Money was put far ahead of doing even the most meagre justice, even the simple matter of taking time for due process.

Equity should have been done, but iniquity was wrought.

Updates and further information:

www.kellidudley.com